Therapist Limits
in Person-Centred Therapy

Lisbeth Sommerbeck

PCCS Books

Monmouth

First published 2015

PCCS BOOKS
Wyastone Business Park
Wyastone Leys
Monmouth
NP25 3SR
contact@pccs-books.co.uk
www.pccs-books.co.uk

Therapist Limits in Person-Centred Therapy

British Library Cataloguing in Publication data: a catalogue record for this book is available from the British Library.

ISBN 978 1 906254 81 0

Cover designed in the UK by Old Dog Graphics
Typeset in the UK by Old Dog Graphics
Printed in the UK by ImprintDigital, Exeter, UK

Contents

Introduction   1

Limits of Therapeutic Competence   3

Limits and congruence   3

Limits in the therapist's experience of
    empathic understanding   7

   When feeling out of contact with the client   7

   When the therapist is the target of extreme affects   9

   When the therapist misses a red thread   14

   When empathic understanding is difficult to communicate 15

Limits in the therapist's experience of
    unconditional positive regard   16

   Limits of acceptance and therapist transparency   18

   Helpful ways of thinking that promote acceptance   20

   Contractual limits on unconditional positive regard   21

Limit setting   25

The essence of limit setting in person-centred therapy   25

Some common limit-setting issues   38

   Limits with respect to suicidal behaviour   38

   Limits with respect to violent behaviour   44

   Idiosyncratic limits   45

Contextual Limits   49

A personal history of being a non-expert on clients in
an expert's setting   49

When the therapist is free to practise in a fully
person-centred way   51

Assessing and diagnosing   61

The end of being a non-expert on clients in an
expert's setting   65

The insidious contagion of contextual rules   66

Limits on the number of sessions   68

Limits as 'Time Out'   71

Limits to answering client questions   72

Limits to therapist self-expression   85

Limits to extra-therapeutic relationships with clients   88

Limits and Referrals   97

Closing Comments   103

References   105

Index   109

Dedication

To all the participants on the former CCT/PCA and current PCINTL (see p. 22) e-mail networks. Without the inspiration I received from our discussions this book would never have materialised.

Acknowledgement

I am very grateful to Pete Sanders of PCCS Books, who edited my manuscript. The result is a strengthening and clarification of expression while, at the same time, leaving more space for readers to do their own thinking and pointing to more issues of discussion. Combining those two trends is no small accomplishment and it has created a more 'reader-centred' book than it was at the start. Pete has also been a paragon of patience in turning my Danish/English language into proper English. Finally, Pete has contributed many useful and thoughtful additions, and he has ensured that the British context of counselling is not neglected by my Danish point of departure. In an important sense Pete is a second author of this book, but of course the responsibility for all of it is mine.

Introduction

Practising person-centred therapy can be difficult, for many reasons. One issue that is frequently brought to supervision is when the therapist's limits are challenged. Surprisingly, there is very little in the client-centred literature about therapist limits in counselling and psychotherapy in relation to adult clients. Much more has been written about therapist limits in work with children (see for example Dorfman, 1951; Axline, 1969; Ellinwood & Raskin, 1993; Moon, 2001), even though the issue of limits is certainly as important in therapy with adults as it is with children.

What little has been written about therapist limits in individual person-centred therapy with adults is quickly surveyed. The most extensive discussion of therapist limits I have found in the literature is by Rogers (1942) in *Counseling and Psychotherapy,* where he devotes a whole section to 'The Matter of Limits' (ibid: 95–108).

In Rogers' next book, *Client-Centered Therapy* (Rogers, 1951: 211), there is just a footnote about setting limits in individual therapy with adults, and some comments about limits in group therapy and education. Apart from this, *Client-Centered Therapy* contains a chapter about play therapy by Elaine Dorfman, with several pages about limits, which seem to be an expansion of Rogers' view (Dorfman 1951: 257–62). Thus it is probably the closest to an extensive discussion of therapist limits in client-centred therapy, as Rogers apparently did not discuss this issue in any of his later works, except for essentially repeating his 1951 footnote in a paper about transference in 1987 (p. 187).

Gendlin (1967: 397–8) has a short section about limits; Lietaer (1993: 40–1) touches on the subject and the term 'limits' is indexed in Barrett-Lennard's book about Rogers' theories, but it only refers to a few lines (Barrett-Lennard, 1998: 66).

Finally, Brodley (1975/2011: 45) has written a short section about boundaries between therapeutic relationships and extra-therapeutic relationships with clients. I (Sommerbeck, 2003: 38–48, 55–6; 2012) have written about the way external factors or the therapist's working context can impose limits on clinical work with clients, and Harrison (2011) has dealt implicitly with limits in a short article on 'non-imposition'.

There are two specific kinds of limits and limit setting that have been discussed comprehensively and explicitly in the person-centred literature: that of referrals as a consequence of therapist limits (Sanders, 2011: 113–20; Sanders, Frankland & Wilkins, 2009: 247–53) and that of time limits in connection with brief person-centred therapy (Shlien, 1957; Tudor, 2008). Nevertheless I'll also discuss these limits briefly in the present book with a particular focus on the controversies inherent in them.

Given the importance of this subject to most therapists, this meagre yield of opinion and discussion on the topic of limits in the person-centred literature is my rationale for writing this book. It is a brief summary of my learning from a long career practising as a person-centred counsellor in various psychiatric settings where I constantly came up against these varied limits in many different manifestations. It started as a chapter for *Person-centred Practice at the Difficult Edge* (Pearce & Sommerbeck, 2014) but outgrew those confines. It will, I hope, help others working today in similar contexts and facing similar challenges in a worsening political, social and therapeutic climate, certainly in the Western world.

In this book I will discuss various kinds of limits, drawn from my own experience as a classical person-centred practitioner:

- limits in the therapist's competence with respect to experiencing and communicating empathic understanding and unconditional acceptance
- limits inherent, explicitly or implicitly, in the therapist's working context
- limits to answering questions
- limits to therapist self-disclosure
- limits to extra-therapeutic relationships with clients
- limits that are idiosyncratic to the individual therapist.

In practice, or course, these kinds of limits influence each other but, for the purposes of this book, it is clearer to deal with them separately.

Limits of Therapeutic Competence

The most central competence of person-centred therapists is their capacity to congruently experience unconditional positive regard for and empathic understanding of the client (Rogers, 1959). Sometimes, however, therapists can reach their limit of this capacity. Here I am going to discuss limits in the therapist's experience of empathic understanding of the client and then look at limits in their experience of unconditional positive regard for the client. In practice this is ordinarily *one* experience; it is only in theory and for clarity's sake that the two can be dealt with as separate. An analogy can be drawn with water: water cannot be separated into oxygen and hydrogen and still be water, but it makes sense to discuss the two elements separately.

Before doing so, however, I want to explore the issue of congruence in relation to limits, and whether it is indeed possible to reconcile the two: can one be fully congruent while working within limits?

Limits and congruence

Particularly in classical client-centred therapy ('Rogers-1 therapy' (Frankel & Sommerbeck, 2005; 2007a) or the therapy described by Rogers in Chapter 2 of *Client-Centered Therapy* (1951: 19–64)), the therapist is supposed to experience and communicate unconditional positive regard for and empathic understanding of the client, and nothing else. Distractions from and disturbances of this experience and communication can thus be regarded as limits on the therapist's capacity in this kind of person-centred work. However, in the variations of person-centred therapy that have taken the work of Rogers-2 as their inspiration, the notion of therapist congruence has led to inclusion of responses from the therapist's own frame of reference. A famous quote from the later Rogers illustrates this:

> I find that when I am the closest to my inner, intuitive self
> – when perhaps I am somehow in touch with the unknown
> in me – when perhaps I am in a slightly altered state of
> consciousness in the relationship. Then whatever I do

seems to be full of healing. Then simply my presence is releasing and helpful. At those moments, it seems that my inner spirit has reached out and touched the inner spirit of the other. Our relationship transcends itself, and has become part of something larger. Profound growth and healing are present. (Baldwin, 2000: 36)

And in the introduction to the interview with Gloria in *Three Approaches to Psychotherapy*, Rogers says:

When I am real in this fashion (genuine) I know that my own feelings will bubble up into awareness but be expressed in ways that won't impose themselves on my client. (Shostrom, 1965)

However, therapists would do well to wonder whether their genuine self-disclosures might impose them on – and therefore possibly negatively influence – their client, since it would be difficult to predict how clients might experience such self-disclosures. Also, as we shall see below, it is questionable whether it is possible for a therapist to tell when he or she is genuine/congruent and when this is not the case.

For Mearns and Cooper, therapist congruence is the core of 'working at relational depth'. They offer a working definition of relational depth as being:

A state of profound contact and engagement between two people, in which each person is fully real with the Other and able to understand and value the Other's experience at a high level. (2005: xii)

From Mearns' transcripts of dialogue that illustrates what it means for the therapist to be 'fully real' with the client, it appears that setting limits on client behaviour can be one way of achieving it, although Mearns and Cooper do not use the term 'limits'. Here is an example from Mearns' session with Dominic (ibid: 77):

Dominic 10: Big question. Maybe I'll need another vodka before I can answer that.

Dave 10: Dom, *be* here, be here *drunk*, but don't play fucking games with me. Neither you nor I deserve that.

Dominic 13: I'm sorry

Dave 13: Apology accepted...

In common with this, most authors seem to subsume the question of therapist limits under the headings of therapists 'being congruent', 'being themselves', 'being real' and so on.

For example, Lietaer writes in a 1993 chapter, 'Authenticity, Congruence and Transparency':

> Finally, we should always take care in maintaining the process sufficiently client-centred and making it a 'self-revelation without imposition'. This can best be done by letting the influencing occur as openly as possible. Two 'rules of communication' should be remembered here. The first one, to use Rogers' words, is 'owning' or giving I-messages instead of you-messages: the therapist indicates clearly that he is the source of the experience and tries above all to communicate what he himself feels, rather than making evaluative statements about the client. He will, for example, not say 'How intrusive of you' but 'When you called me for the second time this week, I felt put under pressure and as if taken possession of...' The second rule of communication is, in Gendlin's words, 'always checking' or 'openness to what comes next': after each intervention – and especially after one which originated in our own frame of reference – tuning in anew to the client's experiential track and continuing from there. (Lietaer, 1993: 40–41)

Therapist self-revelation or intervention originating in their own frame of reference seems in this quotation to be a case of therapist limits with respect to telephone calls from the client, even if the term 'limits' is not mentioned but subsumed under the headings of authenticity, congruence and transparency.

This assumption that the topic of limits is taken care of by reference to congruence is probably the main reason that so little has been written explicitly about therapist limits in the person-centred literature. If the therapist is congruent, expressions from the therapist's frame of reference, including the expression of limits, will by definition be therapeutic. In essence: be congruent, and limits pose no problem! But this assumption seems to me to be precarious at best and at worst mistaken. This is because therapists have no way of knowing whether they are congruent or not and so they cannot know whether their experience of limits in their relationship with a client is a consequence of their being congruent or not.

Rogers (1959: 214) wrote that therapist congruence means that,

> ... the therapist's symbolization of his own experience in the relationship must be accurate, if therapy is to be most effective. Thus if he is experiencing threat and discomfort in the relationship, and is aware only of an acceptance and understanding, then he is not congruent in the relationship and therapy will suffer. It seems important that he should accurately 'be himself' in the relationship, whatever the self of that moment may be.

Rogers, however, offered no criteria for discriminating between accurately symbolised experiences and inaccurately symbolised experiences. Indeed, he also wrote (1959: 210), when discussing internalised conditions of worth, that 'an experience may be perceived as organismically satisfying, when in fact this is not true'. Thus, an experience can be perceived as congruent (meaning that it is organismically satisfying because it maintains or enhances the organism), while the truth is that it is incongruent. This is consistent with Rogers' view that unconscious defence mechanisms (repression, rationalization, distortion, denial) protect the person from awareness of experiences that threaten the self-concept (Rogers, 1959: 229). Then the whole concept of congruence, however, becomes moot and useless as there are no criteria to discriminate between congruent experiences and incongruent experiences.

The impossibility for therapists to know whether their experiences are congruent or not is the main reason it might be mistaken to subsume the topic of therapist limits under the heading of congruence.[1] Accordingly, when students and trainees (and even experienced therapists), bring the issue of limits up in supervision, consultation or workshops because they have serious concerns about it in their relationship with a client, it is dismissive to tell them that it all depends on their being congruent, that the issue will be resolved by their 'being themselves'. Such a response does not take concerns about limits seriously.

Another reason to question subsuming the topic of therapist limits under the heading of 'congruence' is that it is not possible for a therapist to be congruent throughout all of the time they are

---

1. The concept of 'congruence' is problematic in other ways too, which are, however, tangential to the focus of this book. Interested readers are referred to Frankel & Sommerbeck, 2005.

in sessions with their clients. The idea of being congruent or fully functioning is, as Rogers wrote (1959: 235), an ideal. It is a limit, an 'asymptote', which a person can approach very closely but never reach.

Finally, suggesting that students and others 'be congruent' when they are concerned about their limits as therapists individualises their problems – but these are problems they have in common with many other therapists, because the issue of limits is influenced by myriad factors apart from the personality of the individual therapist – not least the influence of their working context. The individual therapist's concern with limits must also be understood from the perspective of the situation in which this concern arises. Marvin Frankel (personal communication, February, 2008) says: 'Individuals are embodiments of their groups. Thus, intrapersonal conflicts are in effect conflicts between groups.' An example is a therapist embodying the conflicts between the group of person-centred therapists and the group of helpers in the psychiatric system.

Limits in the therapist's experience of empathic understanding

There are a number of situations when there may be limits to the therapist's experience of empathic understanding.

When feeling out of contact with the client

Rogers said (1959: 210) that 'being empathic is to perceive the *internal* frame of reference of another with accuracy…' (my italics). Thus empathic understanding means that the therapist understands something of what goes on *beneath* the skin of the client. However, at the 'difficult edge',[2] therapists often experience clients as being 'out of contact', meaning that they have no idea what is going on beneath the client's skin, no idea of the client's *inner* world or internal frame of reference. Instead clients appear withdrawn, talk to themselves or seem emotionally overwhelmed. The first two are common in clients with a diagnosis of psychosis, autism or dementia, and any client, even the least disturbed, can be temporarily emotionally overwhelmed. In these conditions clients are unable to, or uninterested in, making themselves understood by the therapist, who therefore has no sense

---

2. A term taken from Pearce & Sommerbeck (eds) (2014) to mean work in settings or with clients where one or more factors make therapy more difficult: for example, work with clients who have unusual distressing experiences that might be diagnosed as psychosis.

of 'empathic mutuality' with the client and most likely feels at a loss and rather helpless as far as empathic understanding is concerned. Therapists can easily feel they have come to the limit of their capacity in these cases because they find themselves unable to do what they are most used to do and most practised in doing – namely, understanding the client empathically.

Rogers and his co-workers had this experience on the Wisconsin Project when they researched client-centred therapy with people diagnosed with schizophrenia (Rogers et al, 1967). They had been used to a 'neurotic' client population at the Chicago Counseling Center and now they were faced with something quite different: withdrawn and unmotivated clients who had no idea of what psychotherapy was about. Rogers wrote (ibid: 68–69):

> To be consistently rejected, over and over, to be unable to do anything helpful, to see no progress over long periods of time, to see no sign in the patient that he has any understanding of the relationship, *to desire very much to be in touch with this person and to be unable to get through* – these added together constituted a devastating experience. (My italics)

'To desire very much to be in touch with this person and to be unable to get through' is, in my experience, a very precise description of the therapist's experience when reaching the limits of their capacity for empathic understanding.

American psychologist Garry Prouty developed what he termed 'pre-therapy' in the 1980s. His stroke of genius was to develop a therapeutic mode that allows therapists to relate with clients in a truly person-centred way when they have reached their limits in empathic understanding of the client's *inner* frame of reference (Prouty, 1994). This occurs in pre-therapy when the therapist's 'contact reflections' are attuned to the observable surface, not to the client's internal frame of reference – to the client's observable facial expressions, bodily gestures, words and immediate situational surroundings and not to what may be going on beneath their skin, as would occur in regular empathic understanding responses (Prouty, Van Werde & Pörtner, 2002; Sanders, 2007).

The therapists in the Wisconsin Project, however, had no access to pre-therapy, which was developed many years after the project finished; but today's therapists certainly do. I would argue that knowledge of and competence in pre-therapy are essential for any person-centred therapist – indeed, arguably, for therapists of all orientations. Increasingly therapists working in a wide variety of contexts, including student counselling services, voluntary agencies and in private practice, find contact-impaired clients (for whom pre-therapy was developed) turning up in their counselling room. It is also a mistake to assume that relatively well-functioning clients will remain so throughout the course of therapy. Clients who appear to be functioning well at the start of therapy can begin to experience the loss of contact with the therapist, for a variety of reasons, and this is when the therapist often finds that her or she has reached the limits of their capacity for empathic understanding. Sometimes quite 'ordinary' clients in acute crisis will become emotionally overwhelmed, and the therapist may lose a sense of mutuality in the relationship.

Pre-therapy is, *par excellence*, the way to deal with this limit. Before I learned about pre-therapy, I knew there were clients in the back wards of psychiatry with whom I was unable to work. It was a great joy to be able to approach these clients pre-therapeutically, to know that there were no longer clients who were beyond (my) therapeutic reach – at least not through any limits to my empathic understanding.

When the therapist is the target of extreme affects

Clients can experience and express relatively extreme emotions towards the therapist. Whether these emotions are positive or negative, they can present a particular challenge to the therapist's capacity for empathic understanding. Therapists can easily become overly emotionally involved in these situations, or conversely they can withdraw emotionally from the interaction with the client. In the first case, accuracy of empathic understanding tends to be diminished by being tainted with the therapist's own emotional 'stuff'; in the second, their expressions of empathic understanding tend to become mechanical, wooden, 'parrot like'.

These extreme emotions often lie on the devaluation–idealisation dimension of how we experience others. We can idealise them, see them in an unrealistically positive light, and find them faultless. We tend to do this when we fall in love. We can also devalue them, see them as utterly useless and even evil, and be blind to any nuances that would tell a more positive story. We tend to do that when we feel intimidated or threatened by others. Clients can mock and ridicule the therapist, and particularly the therapist's competence, in a way that gets under the skin of even the most experienced therapist. In the face of relentless ridicule, it is understandable that the therapist might feel defensive or devalued. Clients can also express extreme admiration for the therapist, and it can be hard not to 'fall for it' – not to believe that he or she is indispensable, the only one who is able to understand and help the client. Alternatively, the therapist can feel awkward about receiving any praise at all – almost ashamed to empathise with it to its full degree – and inject a measure of sobering modesty in their response to the client.

No therapist, however experienced and competent, is immune to reactions along these lines, particularly when the extreme emotions continue for a long time. Rogers' (1959: 211) distinction between empathising with the client and identifying with the client can be very hard to uphold in these cases. With clients who devalue you, it can be helpful to remember all the clients you *have* helped. With clients who idealise you, it can be helpful to remember other idealising clients who have had a similar tendency to idealise many people. You may be able to hold your sense of awkwardness at bay by remembering that empathic understanding is about understanding not just the *content* but also the *intensity* and extreme range of a client's emotions. However, these rules of thumb are only superficial: peer support and consultation is a must if we are to avoid getting stuck or tangled up in relationships with emotionally extreme clients that become less and less therapeutic, where we lose sight of what we are supposed to be doing, lose sight of our own limits, lose respect for ourselves and our clients, and instead feel increasingly burdened and restricted in our work with them.

Like everyone else, therapists fluctuate in their levels of competence and these fluctuations tend to be more marked when they are the target of extreme emotions. Sometimes the therapist's work is absolutely brilliant; sometimes it is less than his or her usual level of competence. Carl Rogers' own practice was no exception. The following two examples of dialogue show Rogers responding, first, with warmth and accuracy of empathic understanding to a very aggressively devaluing client who seems to be on the brink of psychosis. But in the second, he appears rather withdrawn and mechanical in his responses to a client from the Wisconsin Project, diagnosed with schizophrenia, who mocks and ridicules his competence in a more subtle and composed way, which may have been harder to work with.

Client: (... begins to talk in hard flat voice, quite unlike her usual tone. Does not look at counselor...) You feel I want to come, but I don't! I'm not coming anymore. It doesn't do any good. I don't like you. I hate you! I wish you were never born.

Rogers: You just hate me very bitterly.

Client: I think I'll throw you in the lake. I'll cut you up! You think people like you, but they don't... You think you can attract women but you can't... I wish you were *dead.*

Rogers: You detest me and you'd really like to get rid of me.

Client: You think my father did bad things with me, but he didn't! You think he wasn't a good man, but he *was.* You think I want intercourse but I *don't.*

Rogers: You feel that I *absolutely misrepresent* all your thoughts.

Client: ... You think you can get people to come in and tell you everything, and they'll think they're being helped, but they're *not.* You just like to make 'em suffer. You think you can hypnotize them, but you *can't*! You think you're good, but you ain't. I hate you. I *hate* you.

Rogers: You feel I really like to make 'em suffer, but I don't help them.

Client: You think I haven't been straight, but I have. I *hate* you. All I've had is pain, pain, pain. You think I can't direct my own life, but I can. You think I can't get well, but I can. You think I had hallucinations, but I didn't. I hate you. (Long pause, leans on desk in strained, exhausted pose.) You think I'm crazy but I'm not.

Rogers: You're sure I think you're crazy.

Client: (Pause) I'm tied, and I just can't get loose! (Despairing tone of voice and tears. Pause) I had a hallucination and I've got to get it out! (Goes on about her deep conflicts, and tells of the hallucination she has experienced, with terrific tension in her voice, but with an attitude very different from that at the beginning of the interview.)

[Later in interview...]

Client: I knew at the office I had to get rid of this somewhere. I felt I could come down and tell you. I knew you'd understand. I couldn't say I hated myself. That's true but I couldn't say it. So I just thought of all the ugly things I could say to you instead.

Rogers: The things you felt about yourself you couldn't say, but you could say them to me.

Client: I know we're coming to rock bottom (Rogers, 1951: 211–13)

In a footnote Rogers writes:

> Just as it is impossible to convey on paper the venom and hatred in the client's voice, so it is utterly impossible to convey the depth of empathy in the counselor's[3] responses. The counselor states, 'I tried to enter into and to express in my voice the full degree of soul-consuming anger which she was pouring out. The written words look incredibly pale, but in the situation they were full of the same feeling she was so coldly and deeply expressing'. (Ibid: 212)

Evidently this was a very fruitful interview.

Here is the second example, taken from the fifth interview with this client:[4]

Client: Have you had experience working with people where drinking is the problem?

(Long pause)

Rogers: I'm trying to sort of see what my feelings are in response to that. The factual answer to your question is easy enough. The factual answer is simply, 'some'. But I also find myself feeling something beyond that. The feeling is, I am just whatever I am in this relationship.

Client: What does that mean?

Rogers: I guess it means nothing to you, so let's skip it.

Client: You kind of put me on the defensive. I feel as though it isn't right somehow for me to ask questions of you – as though you aren't willing for me or don't want me to ask you questions. And yet these questions are vital to me.

Rogers: I guess it seems to you that somehow I'm not really receptive to the things you want to ask and yet they're damned significant to you.

---

3. In this case, Rogers' own responses.
4. The client did not allow the interviews to be recorded, so the transcript is based on the notes Rogers wrote after the sessions. Bill Coulson, who kept the Wisconsin transcripts for Rogers, kindly presented me with a copy of these notes, titled 'Carl Rogers' reconstruction of his first Wisconsin case'.

There follow some exchanges about their mutual lack of knowledge about each other, and then the fifth interview ends as follows:

> Client: You say you don't know anything of me. You're ignorant of me. You're ignorant about me. You don't seem to want to take any steps to remedy that ignorance. I don't know you. I'm ignorant about you. How could anything happen in a situation like that?
>
> Rogers: I guess you feel that it's kind of an *impasse* which has similarities on both sides. I have no knowledge of you. I don't seem to be taking action to remedy that. You feel equally lacking in knowledge about me: and so how could anything come of it?
>
> Client: I say something my way, and then you say it your way. It's just fascinating that I try to say something and then you put it in your words. It's just like an echo chamber.
>
> (Long pause)
>
> Rogers: I see our time is up for today. Friday?
>
> Client: (After long pause) Put up or shut up. (Long pause) Okay.

The following is from the seventh and last interview (the client had actually wanted to stop seeing Rogers, but Rogers had asked him to come for this interview):

> Client: I don't understand why I'm here this morning.
>
> Rogers: As far as I'm concerned, I simply asked if you would come and you have come and I appreciate that.
>
> Client: I've done you a favor, is that it?
>
> Rogers: Yes, and I appreciate it.
>
> Client: So you're obligated to me?
>
> Rogers: No, I feel no sense of obligation. I asked you to come in, you did, and I appreciated it; I told you things I wanted to express to you.
>
> Client: Then you feel no sense of obligation?
>
> Rogers: No
>
> Client: Do you know anything more about me than you did when I last saw you?
>
> Rogers: No, would you like me to?
>
> Client: I won't answer that.
>
> Rogers: I must seem to you like a pretty strange duck, not even

> finding out about you from the record and so on.
>
> Client: No, you're not strange; I find you very usual... Well, I've done my favor, I guess I can go.
>
> Rogers: I appreciate your coming in, and I would like to see you a week from today at this same time if you're willing, so that we can get together for several casual contacts, so that we could get to know each other better in order that in time you could really decide whether you wanted to continue it or not. You don't need to answer that now, however, unless you wish.
>
> Client: I'm willing to answer that now, and the answer is no.

He got up to leave the room and Rogers said 'Goodbye' and the client said 'Goodbye'.

This may well be one of the clients Rogers was thinking of when he wrote in a footnote (Rogers et al, 1967: 26) that he regretted not having correlated for client motivation in the Wisconsin Project.

When the therapist misses a 'red thread'

Most therapists associate empathic understanding with the ability to follow the 'red thread'[5] in the client's narrative. This, of course, means that therapists expect to find a red thread; however with many clients this cannot be assumed: experienced therapists know that clients very rarely meet therapists' expectations. The remedy is to lower one's expectations of being able to follow a red thread. The client may seem to jump incomprehensibly from one point to another. In such cases the therapist needs to have great tolerance for their own 'not-understanding'. They may understand in bits and pieces, but they must tolerate the fact that they cannot see any connection between these bits and pieces. What the client says can seem very fragmented and, in following this, the therapist's responses will be fragmented too; one response will be dissociated from the preceding response and from the one that follows. Therapy with these clients is an exercise *par excellence* in 'holding and letting go': the therapist needs to let go of their understanding of the present moment in order to follow the client's next move, even if it seems to contradict the one preceding it. Rogers described similar processes in relation to unconditional positive regard: 'It involves ... as much acceptance of ways he [the

---

5. A 'red thread' is a Danish figure of speech meaning the logical sequence of something interwoven in a narrative.

client] is inconsistent as of ways in which he is consistent' (Rogers, 1957: 98).

When empathic understanding is difficult to communicate

Some clients talk to themselves in a fast, seemingly endless stream of associations, apparently under a huge pressure to talk. If the therapist wants to do their job to follow and understand these clients empathically, they may need to interrupt the client's stream of talking quite forcefully by urgently and insistently saying something along the lines of: 'Wait a minute, let me see if I have understood you...' If they don't, they are likely to be left totally behind and, in the process, come to feel increasingly out of contact with the client. But if they insist on doing their job of trying to understand, they will experience increased mutuality in their contact with the client. They will also experience an increase in the client's interest in the contact. It is as if these clients slowly realise that the therapist truly wants to understand them and is not out to correct them or silence them.

Interrupting a client's fast-streaming monologue in this way may, superficially, seem like a violation of the principle of non-directivity, but on a deeper level it means that the therapist stays with the client. The client is not abandoned by the therapist giving up trying to follow them and instead just letting their words pass in through one ear and out through the other.

For Barbara Brodley (1998: 25), this situation – 'When the therapist feels an impulse or desire to express and communicate his or her self while immersed in the attempt to empathically understand' – is one of five criteria for making tentative empathic understanding responses (EURs). She goes on:

> This impulse or desire to express oneself, which is resolved through expression of understandings, probably originates in the interpersonal and interactional nature of the psychotherapeutic relation. Inherent in an interpersonal relation is an expectation of an exchange – a back and forth characteristic of the interaction. The deeply empathically engaged therapist, however, seldom will experience any specific content from his or her own frame of reference that could serve as a vehicle for self-expression. Thus, when the interaction involves almost exclusive focus and attention on the client member of the

dyad, the therapist may feel the desire to be responsive and expressive through the vehicle of tentative empathic understandings.

Limits in the therapist's experience of unconditional positive regard

All therapists now and then experience fluctuations in their unconditional positive regard for or unconditional acceptance of the client. Rogers wrote in a footnote (1957: 98):

> The phrase 'unconditional positive regard' may be an unfortunate one, since it sounds like an absolute, an all or nothing dispositional concept. It is probably evident from the description that completely unconditional positive regard would never exist except in theory. From a clinical and experiential point of view I believe the most accurate statement is that the effective therapist experiences unconditional positive regard for the client during many moments of his contact with him, yet from time to time he experiences only a conditional positive regard – and perhaps at times a negative regard, though this is not likely in effective therapy. It is in this sense that unconditional positive regard exists as a matter of degree in any relationship.

It is of course comforting to know that Rogers acknowledged that the level of unconditional acceptance of the client will necessarily fluctuate. Nevertheless, the degree of fluctuation in unconditional acceptance can be so marked that it is painful for therapists and hard for them to endure. This is especially apparent when it is a matter of *negative* regard, which is certainly likely to occur with some clients, even when the outcome of therapy is positive. Experienced therapists often bring to supervision this issue of negative regard for their client and it is an issue that students frequently ask about in training.

For example, with the focus in recent years on paedophilia and offering therapy to paedophiles, students frequently say that they feel it would be impossible for them to experience unconditional positive regard for such clients. Here they experience a limit that they feel unable, and sometimes unwilling, to transcend, out of sheer abhorrence of the particular crime. A therapist should be able to choose not to work with a particular client group if they do not wish to do so. However, there are ways of thinking that can promote unconditional positive regard for the paedophile client, as well as for other clients whose behaviour repels us (I discuss this further below).

Drawing from my own experience of fluctuating positive regard, I recall the day after the 9/11 attacks on the US, when my colleagues and I shared our horror at our usual 'morning briefing'. We had all been sitting glued to the television late into the night and early hours of the morning. We agreed that we all felt a need to mark this sad day by flying the flag at half-mast on the lawn outside and keeping a minute's silence while doing so. In this mood of sadness we separated to start the day's work.

I went to my office to meet my first client that day. As she entered the room, she looked out of the window and exclaimed: 'But the flag shouldn't be half-mast! It should be all up! This is a wonderful day: now America has been taught the lesson it has deserved for ages; it is a reason for jubilation, not for sadness' – and continued to the same effect. She spoke in the same rather shrill tone of voice that I had heard on television the night before when I had witnessed with horror the scenes of jubilation in the streets of Gaza.

I was completely taken aback and, as she spoke, my previous acceptance of her changed to loathing – I actually felt like throwing her out of the room! I was close to panicking, feeling like this, so utterly anti-therapeutic, and I toyed for some seconds with the idea of making an excuse to cancel our session – a sudden headache or something like that. Then I took a very firm grip on myself, telling myself that I was not supposed to be her judge, nor a political discussion partner, nor a teacher, indeed – nothing but her therapist, and that this meant trying to understand her empathically. All this whirled around in my mind in the space of a few seconds, so when we settled down in our chairs I was firmly decided on putting my own perspective as far away as possible in order to concentrate on hers. In the first minutes of the session this was no small struggle; I was not nearly as present in our interaction as I would normally have been, and my empathic understanding responses were certainly rather 'wooden'. Nevertheless, she responded with further exploration of her experience, and consequently I did indeed, as Rogers wrote in 1967 (see quotation p. 20), start to understand more of the meaning and value of her thoughts to her, and to understand how they were a natural consequence of her experiences and her background. In this process my acceptance of her slowly returned to its ordinary level and I could again be fully present with her. My loathing had evaporated.

Limits of acceptance and therapist transparency

Because of my critical view of the concept of congruence (see pp. 3–7) I prefer to understand this concept as 'comfortable transparency', meaning that the therapist does not try to withhold from the client what is going on for them (the therapist). What the therapist expresses to the client matches what is going on in him or her as it is experienced, and the therapist feels comfortable with this transparency. What about such transparency in the case I just described? Obviously I was not transparent with the client in the first minutes of the session, because I did all I could to hide my experience from my client. But I felt more comfortable doing so because, to feel comfortable, I must primarily feel that what I do is *therapeutically relevant* to the client: that I am doing the best I can *as a therapist* – and nothing else but as a therapist. That feeling of being therapeutically relevant first came to me with my decision to struggle for empathic understanding. And while I did that, I also tried to hide my struggle from the client, since my struggle to become fully present with her seemed to me to be therapeutically irrelevant. I expected this perturbed state to pass away relatively quickly, and it did. Thus, my wish to be transparent and my wish to be relevant can sometimes get into conflict, and many therapists might recognise this conflicting state of affairs. But what about when this struggle for positive regard does not resolve quickly?

The concept of being congruent is of no help here. Is a public speaker who does their best to hide their nervousness at the start of the speech because they believe telling their audience about it is irrelevant to the task at hand less 'congruent' than the speaker who discloses their nerves? Your answer might depend on your views about therapist self-disclosure in therapy. A more conservative position would suggest that therapist self-disclosure is always 'therapist-centred', not client-centred, and therefore non-therapeutic. Thus, even when not fully present with the client due to an internal struggle with judgmentalism, a sustained effort at empathic understanding is more likely to be successful and in many cases will help the therapist regain the experience of unconditional acceptance of the client.

If the diminution of the therapist's experience of unconditional acceptance turns out to be more persistent, it is time for consultation or supervision. As a last resort, therapists may find it necessary to share their experiences with the client in order to clear the space, and in the hope that the client will understand that the experiences of the therapist belong to the therapist and do not necessarily reflect on the client. The disclosure may, or may not, turn out to be therapeutic for the client, and the risk inherent in therapist self-disclosure is greater when working with more distressed clients. For example in a psychiatric context, these clients normally have a more externalised locus of evaluation and are thus more likely to sniff out conditional regard from a therapist's self-disclosures – and less likely to understand that the therapist's experiences do not necessarily reflect on them.

Therapists inevitably vary in the degree of self-disclosure they find relevant and acceptable, and as mentioned above, in some forms of person-centred therapy, therapist self-disclosures are much more prominent than in others. In practice, there is probably a continuum at play here.

Rogers (1959: 214) had this answer to the question of therapist self-disclosures:

> Should he also express or communicate to the client the accurate symbolization of his own experience? The answer to this question is still in an uncertain state. At present we would say that such feelings should be expressed, if the therapist finds himself persistently focused on his own feelings rather than those of the client, thus greatly reducing or eliminating any experience of empathic understanding, or if he finds himself persistently experiencing some feeling other than unconditional positive regard.

Whether 'accurately symbolised' or not (recalling the lack of criteria for discriminating between accurate and inaccurate symbolisation (see p. 6)), Rogers' point is that there is a great likelihood that the therapist's *persistent* feeling of conditional regard will be perceived by the client, whereas they are much less likely to notice fleeting instances of such experiences. Readers will be able to judge from their own experience whether this appears to be true.

Helpful ways of thinking that promote acceptance

It is often said that unconditional acceptance is acceptance of the essential humaneness of the client, not of the behaviour of the client. In this vein, Barrett-Lennard (1998: 66) says that limit setting is 'on behavior, not on attitudes and feelings'. Rogers, however, seemed doubtful about this. He wrote (Rogers et al, 1967: 103–4):

> The question is often raised: But what about the therapist's attitude toward his client's asocial or antisocial behavior? Is he to accept this without evaluation? Sometimes this question is answered by saying that the effective therapist prizes the person, but not necessarily his behavior. Yet it is doubtful if this is an adequate or true answer. To be sure, the therapist may feel that a particular behavior is socially unacceptable or socially bad, something he could not approve of in himself, and a way of behaving which is inimical to the welfare of the social group. But the effective therapist may feel acceptant of this behavior in his client, not as desirable behavior, but as a *natural consequence* of the circumstances, experiences, and feelings of this client. Thus the therapist's acceptance may be based upon this kind of feeling: 'If I had had the same background, the same circumstances, the same experiences, it would be inevitable in me, as it is in this client, that I would act in this fashion' ...
>
> Thus when the therapist prizes his client, and is searching for the meaning or value of his client's thoughts or behaviors within the client, he does not tend to feel a response of approval or disapproval. He feels an acceptance of what *is*.

This quotation may be helpful for practitioners who experience momentary dips in unconditional acceptance of the client, as I describe above in the case of my client after 9/11.

There is still another way of thinking that can be helpful in maintaining unconditional positive regard for the client. When a therapist enjoys the interaction with the client, they may have a sense of liking the client, and thus unconditional acceptance comes rather easily: we tend to like a person when we enjoy our interactions with them. But this sense of *liking* the client may be treacherous. It is context dependent. Would the therapist have liked the client if they had happened to meet at a dinner party, at a political event, as parents of children in the same school class, and so on? In these contexts their interactions might not have been so pleasant, and they might not have had the sense of liking each other. But as far as the therapist's experience of unconditional acceptance of the client goes, it is enough for the therapist to enjoy the interaction with the client in the context of *therapy* – in his or her role as the therapist of this other person in their role as client. (Incidentally, this is one of the reasons it is considered unprofessional/unethical practice to have extra-therapeutic relationships with clients; see pp. 88–95.)

Neither therapist nor client can know how they'd feel about each other outside the context of therapy. It is therefore important for therapists to be confident, in whatever way they can, that they look forward to their next therapy session with the client. This is no more than taking steps to protect their experience of therapeutic freedom and comfort in their relationship with the client. The aim of all the previous discussion in this chapter has been to help therapists do precisely that, and it remains the aim of the discussion of limit setting that follows.

First, though, let's finish this section with another comforting quotation from Rogers (1957: 97), this time about congruence. The quote seemingly implies that congruent experiences, including that of unconditional acceptance of the client, may be context dependent – that is, dependent on the client being precisely that particular client of this particular therapist, and nothing else, as I described above:

> It is not necessary (nor is it possible) that the therapist be a paragon who exhibits this degree of integration, of wholeness, in every aspect of his life. It is sufficient that he is accurately himself in this hour of this relationship, that in this basic sense he is what he actually is, in this moment of time.

Contractual limits on unconditional positive regard

In what we might call 'regular' person-centred therapy with voluntary clients,[6] therapist and client agree a contract specifying time and place for sessions (or, at least, time and place for the next session) and the fee to be paid by the client for the therapist's service.

---

6. With this formulation I am excluding the cases of very contact-impaired clients where the therapist takes the initiative to contact the client, mostly in a pre-therapeutic way.

With respect to fees, John Shlien (personal communication, 2000), half-joking, half-serious, said that to be truly client-centred the therapist has to offer his or her service for free, otherwise unconditional positive regard is not unconditional but dependent on the client paying the fee. For reasons like these, and others, Doug Bower, in messages to the PCINTL e-mail network,[7] has often claimed that unconditional positive regard simply does not exist. He prefers to speak of 'acceptance *regardless* of regard'.

With respect to contracts (agreements about fees and appointments) I think John Shlien and Doug Bower have a point, because it is probably true that a therapist's unconditional positive regard for a client is affected when the client breaks their contract. In this event, to be able to return to experiencing unconditional positive regard for the client, the therapist will most likely need to request 'time out' (see below, pp. 71–96) from therapy in order to negotiate this issue with the client. In this sense it seems true that the unconditional positive regard of most therapists for their clients is, basically, conditional. Unconditional positive regard exists within the frame of both parties being committed to their agreed contract. And clients too may request 'time out' of therapy to (re)negotiate their contract.

I have always worked in the Danish public health system, where clients do not pay for treatment, so have no experience of negotiating fees with clients. I know that many person-centred therapists have a sliding scale according to the client's resources. One, for example, charges per session what the client is paid per hour or receives in benefits. But I can see how in spite of this, contractual problems regarding fees may occur and, for example, the therapist will feel cheated by a client who, having agreed to pay a minimal fee, turns up in brand new clothes; the therapist is likely to experience a drop in unconditional positive regard. If the client does not pay the agreed fee, this will similarly affect the therapist.

With regard to breaches of contract, my own experience of limits to my unconditional positive regard for clients relates to the issue of keeping appointments. I would get into trouble with my manager, and with good reason, if I didn't take action when clients failed to keep their appointments with me without notification. Our

7. The PCINTL e-mail network is an e-mail list dedicated to discussion of person-centred theory and practice. It is managed by Jerold Bozarth and you can join by mailing jeroldbozarth@gmail.com

service had many clients on the waiting list, and it was simply not permissible for my time to be wasted. Therefore I made sure that my outpatient[8] clients were informed that missing appointments without notification might mean the end of therapy. I remember two clients who missed two or three consecutive sessions without notice. I wrote to tell them that I regarded our current contact as ended, but they were of course welcome to go back on the waiting list if they wished. I had no response from either of them.

8. Staff members took care of cancellations from inpatients and day patients.

Limit Setting

The essence of limit setting in person-centred therapy

Rogers (1942: 95–108) wrote, in a section headed 'The Matter of Limits':

> The amateur or untrained counselor, bolstered by good
> intentions, anxious not to hurt the client, has a tendency
> to accede to the requests, to do almost anything which
> the client feels will help, until the demand upon time or
> affection or responsibility grows too great for the counselor
> to bear. Then his affection and desire to help turn to
> avoidance and dislike. He blames the client and rejects
> him. The net result is that the client feels that one more
> person has betrayed him, that one more person who
> claimed to wish to help has actually failed in time of stress.
> He may be definitely and sometimes permanently hurt by
> this bungled attempt at counseling.

Of course, it is not only inexperienced therapists who can exceed their limits like this. It can also happen, often quite inadvertently and/or imperceptibly, to the experienced therapist, and it is important that therapists do not end up in the vicious 'saviour/victim/persecutor' triangle that Rogers described in the quotation above.

It also appears that Rogers, in 1942, thought that limit setting was very much a therapeutic factor in and of itself: limit setting was primarily for the sake of the client. Rogers might well still have been influenced by the dominant psychoanalytic therapy culture of the time, and by his own psychoanalytic training.

In *Client-Centered Therapy* (Rogers, 1951) there is just a footnote about limit setting (p. 211):

> As in setting any limit in the therapeutic experience, this
> is something which is purely the responsibility of the
> therapist, and he takes that responsibility. He does not
> attempt to evaluate the client's experience by some such
> statement as 'That really wouldn't help you.' He simply

takes responsibility for his own behavior, at the same time indicating understanding and acceptance of the client's experience of the situation.

Here, in 1951, Rogers has evidently changed his perspective from 1942; limit setting is no longer therapeutic in and of itself: it is not for the sake of the client, but solely for the sake of the therapist.

His footnote is a comment on an example of limit setting (Rogers, 1951: 211) that it might be illustrative to include here, as it is probably characteristic of limit setting in today's person-centred practice:

Client: I think emotionally I'm dying for sexual intercourse but I don't do anything about it... The thing I want is to have sexual intercourse with you. I don't dare ask you, because I'm afraid you'd be nondirective.

Rogers: You have this awful tension, and want so much to have relations with me.

Client: (Goes on in the same vein. Finally) Can't we do something about it? This tension is awful! Will you relieve the tension ... Can you give me a direct answer? I think it might help both of us.

Rogers: (Gently) The answer would be no. I can understand how *desperately* you feel, but I would not be willing to do that.

Client: (Pause; sigh of relief) I think that helps me. It's only when I'm upset that I'm like this. You have strength, and it gives me strength.

Rogers later confirmed his perspective on limit setting in the example above (Rogers, 1987: 187): 'It is noteworthy that when the therapist responds to her question and states his unwillingness (on ethical grounds) to engage in sex, he speaks solely for himself, and of himself.' But, of course, it is not so simple as that. The ethical grounds for the therapist's unwillingness certainly embrace considerations of the client's welfare in the overall course of therapy. In the examples throughout the rest of this book we will often see how the distinction between 'for the sake of the therapist' and 'for the sake of the client' is actually blurred because the therapist sets limits in order to continue as a good therapist for the client – in order to be, eventually, of maximal helpfulness to the client.

As mentioned earlier, the therapists who researched the effect of client-centred therapy on people diagnosed with schizophrenia in the Mendota State Hospital, Wisconsin (Rogers et al, 1967), often had a very difficult time:

> Initially Mrs FIN was very resistant to therapy and, after four interviews, refused to come again. At this point the therapist insisted that Mrs FIN continue but gave her more freedom with the therapeutic hour by explaining that she could leave when overly uncomfortable. A turning point in the relationship occurred when, under the stress of moving to a new ward, Mrs FIN cried and expressed her feelings of aloneness and helplessness to the therapist. Possibly the most meaningful elements in the relationship with Mrs FIN were my nonverbal expressions of concern and caring (seeing her on the ward, loaning my coat to her etc). (Hart & Tomlinson, 1970: 16)

> The patient refused right from the start to meet with me. To every mention of 'next time' and to every invitation to enter a room with me, he reacted with explicit anger and demands that I leave him alone. Over some weeks I accepted his feeling, anger, dislike of me: I let him leave; I had him brought by attendants; I argued with him; I was both honest and dishonest: I could not help but react negatively to his rejection and I felt he cut the ground from under my right to be with him. Because of these feelings in me I decided that he should not be further coerced to see me, since he would only discover a threatened and threatening person in me. How to make the contacts continue – and yet without the sort of coercion which brought this rejection and altered my inward climate? (Hart & Tomlinson, 1970: 16)

These examples describe situations where the therapist's limits and limit setting were challenged and overburdened, sometimes to desperation. However, the topic of limits is never dealt with explicitly in the published work on the Wisconsin Project (Rogers et al, 1967). Just one of the therapists in the Wisconsin research team, Gendlin, wrote a paragraph where he describes limit setting and the attitude that should accompany limit setting in order that it can be potentially therapeutic:

> When we give a client feedback about a behavior which irritates us, we try to get in touch with the needs and positive intentions behind it, and include these in our

> discussion. For example, I might not let a patient touch
> me or grab me. I will stop the patient, but in the same
> words and gesture I will try to respond positively to the
> positive desire for closeness or physical relations. I will
> make personal touch with my hand as I hold the patient
> away from me, contact the patient's eyes, and declare
> that I think the physical reaching out is positive and I
> welcome it, even though I cannot allow it. (I know at such
> times that I may be partly creating this positive aspect.
> Perhaps this reaching is more hostile, right now, than
> warm. But there is warmth and health in anyone's sexual
> or physical need, and I can recognize that as such.)
> (Gendlin, 1967: 397)

The reader may also remember that Lietaer, in the quote in the first chapter of this book (p. 5) offers what might probably be called recommendations or rules for limit setting:

> Two 'rules of communication' should be remembered
> here. The first one, to use Rogers' words, is 'owning' or
> giving I-messages instead of you-messages: the therapist
> indicates clearly that he is the source of the experience
> and tries above all to communicate what he himself
> feels, rather than making evaluative statements about
> the client... The second rule of communication is, in
> Gendlin's words, 'always checking' or 'openness to what
> comes next': after each intervention... tuning in anew to
> the client's experiential track and continuing from there.
> (Lietaer, 1993: 40)

Recently Harrison (2011) has dealt more explicitly, albeit briefly, with limits and limit setting in his work on 'non-imposition' – a term he prefers to 'non-directivity'. Harrison suggests that, by 'offering their limits', the therapist does not impose on the client and ensures that the client does not impose on them:

> My sense is that in offering their limits, the therapist is
> not imposing social conditions of worth, but offering to
> share contact, to be social. The client has the freedom
> to choose whether or not such social conditions are
> acceptable, whether to ignore or negotiate the point, or
> break contact. (Ibid: 7)

It is questionable whether the client has the 'freedom' attributed to them by Harrison. Clients usually feel more dependent on their therapists than vice versa, and it is also worth remembering that person-centred therapy is, in part, an effort to diminish the imbalance of power between therapist and client – the power of the expert over the non-expert. According to Rogers' second condition for therapeutic change (Rogers, 1959: 213), clients are, by definition, incongruent, which means that their locus of evaluation is more or less externalised. In other words, they will have a tendency to regard their therapists as experts on what is wrong with them and what is needed to make them better. This is not a relationship of 'freedom of choice' between client and therapist – on the contrary. And the whole notion of 'freedom to choose', whether for client, therapist or anybody else, is arguable: are we really as free as we sometimes think we are? The freedom/determinism question has been debated for hundreds of years without resolution and the debate will continue, even if Harrison seems to believe that the matter is settled.

In January 2012 I participated in a PCINTL e-mail network discussion (see p. 7) about limits and limit setting. I have permission from some of the participants to quote them here:

Jin Wu wrote:

> The client-centred therapist checks with oneself to see if honoring a client's request would compromise one's ability to provide the conditions, so such limits vary a great deal from therapist to therapist; one might be able to take 3am phone calls, another might not be able to go five minutes longer for the session. In other words, a client-centred therapist has an internal locus of control for setting limits, not necessarily an external standard (beyond what's legal).

Dorothy Morgan wrote:

> I think limits and limit setting would fall within the category of genuineness in that it would be presented as, 'I am unable to follow you there (for whatever reason).' I do think it is important that limits be presented in terms of an inability of the therapist rather than as correct/ incorrect, appropriate/inappropriate etc.

Kathy Moon wrote (quoting from her own article on therapy with children (Moon, 2001: 46–47)):

> I prefer to say that limits are set in the service of the therapist. The purpose is to help the therapist maintain equanimity and positive regard towards the client. Limits are set in the service of the child only because they are necessary to the therapist in order for the therapist to remain acceptant, empathic and congruent. I consider any other purpose for limits to be didactic and contrary to the condition of unconditional positive regard.

I responded to Kathy Moon as follows:

> I guess the essence of the person-centred therapist's limit setting is, as you write, that limit setting is in the service of the therapist or, more specifically perhaps, in the service of the therapist's capacity to remain unconditionally acceptant and empathically understanding of the client.
>
> In a way, I think of it as my putting on warm, windproof and rainproof clothes before going out for a walk at this time of the year in Denmark. In that way I avoid getting freezing wet and instead I can enjoy the weather and cherish all the beautiful nuances of it.

Finally, Jere Moorman asked:

> If a child is ransacking my filing cabinet, for example, it seems to me I can say 'no' and still remain within the protocol of UPR?

And I answered:

> Sure, Jere – I even believe that in order to stay unconditionally acceptant of the child you *need* to say 'no'.

There were other contributions in the same vein, and it thus seems to be a general view that limit setting is for the protection of the therapist's capacity to remain unconditionally acceptant and empathically understanding of the client. In other words, by respecting their own limits, the therapist avoids getting into the saviour/victim/persecutor triangle in their relationship with clients in which the therapist sacrifices their limits in order to 'save' the client. In that scenario, when the client appears unable to cope with the therapist's limit, the therapist, subtly and with little or no awareness, blames (persecutes) the client for his or her ingratitude for their sacrifice and feels a victim of the client's demands. In none of these scenarios is there unconditional positive regard for the client. Unconditional positive regard for the client can only be experienced when the therapist feels free, including free to express their own limits, in their relationship with clients.

Nevertheless, therapists can occasionally end up in this vicious triangle with a client. This happens quite often in psychiatric settings. One solution is for the therapist to apologise to the client for having exceeded their own limits as soon as they become aware that they have, indeed, done so. But this needs to be done explicitly; the therapist must admit they have made a mistake and make clear that the client is not to blame and offer further explanation and discussion. Otherwise the relationship is likely to be harmed by an undercurrent of feelings of regret and restriction on the part of the therapist. It is the therapist's responsibility to regain his or her experience of feeling free in the relationship with the client so they can again experience unconditional positive regard for the client.

As Rogers wrote about limits in 1942, in a paragraph headed 'The value of limits to the therapist':

> ... they allow the counselor to be more comfortable and to function more effectively. They provide a framework within which the counselor can be free and natural in dealing with the client. (Rogers, 1942: 108)

Harrison (2011: 8) apparently goes further when he writes:

> ... when the limits are being reached then the therapist is faced with finding a way of being that maybe *promotes* the ongoing existence of all six of Rogers (1957, 1959) conditions. (My emphasis).

Here is an example from my own practice where I exceed my limits and ended up in the saviour/persecutor/victim triangle with my client, with the predictable harmful effects on our relationship.[1]

---

1. PCCS Books has kindly permitted me to take this example, in a slightly edited version, from my book *The Client-Centred Therapist in Psychiatric Contexts* (Sommerbeck, 2003: 102–103)

I had been seeing Peter in therapy for four years, with sessions at various frequencies, from twice a week to once a month, according to Peter's wishes. Peter had a diagnosis of paranoid psychosis, although a long time had passed since his most recent psychotic episode. He had been hospitalised many times, always on a fully voluntary basis. When I first knew him he was rather withdrawn; later he expressed his psychotic experiences more openly, and around the time of the developments described in this example he was plagued more by suicidal impulses than by psychotic ideation.

Looking back, it is evident to me now that he had progressed a long way in the direction of 'normalcy', which had been his deepest wish all through the years I knew him. Medication had been a necessary evil to him; he had reluctantly accepted disability benefit, and he had consistently refused offers of more protected living facilities than his own flat. He was, though, very motivated for psychotherapy, and when hospitalised he was also engaged positively in various kinds of therapeutic and educational activities on the ward.

He had artistic talents and about a year previously he took the very scary step of entering art school. Later he sold a couple of paintings and was now hoping to become more economically independent as an artist. In addition, he had struggled to keep off medication and he felt convinced that his latest hospitalisation, just before he entered art school, would be the last. In sessions he variously expressed his feelings of trust in his ability to lead an independent life, his feelings of loneliness and of being on the periphery of his group of classmates in art school, and his feelings of being a failure as a man because he didn't know how to relate with women. Such is the context in which he, at the end of a session, asked me if he could phone me between sessions when he became scared that he could no longer control his suicidal impulses.

Ordinarily, I would refuse to accommodate such a request and explain why I didn't want to accommodate it (see comment 6, below). Clients either find other ways of resolving their problem or I suggest an alternative offer that feels comfortable to both of us. At the same time I would respond with empathic understanding of the client's experience of my refusal to accommodate their wishes. In this case, though, without clearly knowing why, but also not feeling fully comfortable with it, I accommodated his request. During the following days he did call me, and, among other things, he expressed both his gratitude that he could call me like this and his assurances that these phone sessions would help him get through his current crisis. However, as time went on, the phone sessions became more frequent and longer, and Peter seemed increasingly disturbed and suicidal. I, too, felt increasingly disturbed about the direction our relationship had taken, and still more disturbed by growing feelings of annoyance at the interruptions in my schedule and anxiety that whether he would end his life or not depended on me. My capacity for experiencing unconditional acceptance and empathic understanding of him had diminished substantially.

I realised I needed help and I recounted my problems with Peter in my peer consultation group. The acceptance and understanding I experienced in the group helped me clarify that I had identified with Peter's wish to avoid hospitalisation because another hospitalisation would feel like a defeat of my psychotherapeutic abilities. Not long ago, I and the staff members of the ward where Peter had been hospitalised so many times shared our pleasure in Peter's progress and the positive effects of psychotherapy since his last hospitalisation. We prophesied that hospitalisation would probably become no longer necessary. This made it harder for me to accept that yet another hospitalisation might be needed. In short, I had identified with one side of Peter's dilemma, to the detriment of the other; in a sense I had colluded with him in denial and non-acceptance of his dependency wishes. My acceptance and empathic understanding of his growing wishes for protection and dependency had been disturbed by my own vanity and narcissistic wishes for a therapeutic 'success' and my own need to feel helpful. As a consequence I had, quite unrealistically, offered myself as protection.

The next time Peter called I was able to discuss these issues with him with acceptance of both our positions, and with concurrent acceptance and empathic understanding of his feelings of being a failure because he once again wanted protection. He also disclosed that he actually did have a sense that I did not feel wholly comfortable about our agreement that he could phone me when he felt he wanted to do so, and that this made him feel quite unsafe in our relationship. So when I apologised for my mistake and expressed my wish to correct it by terminating our 'phone sessions' routine, he reacted with mixed feelings of disappointment, relief and anxiety about what to do the next time he felt hopeless and suicidal. He resolved to make an appointment with his psychiatrist to discuss medication and hospitalisation. The result was that he became a day patient in his old ward twice a week on the days he was not in art school, and I resumed ordinary sessions with him once a week. In these he spoke mostly of his experiences in art school and after a couple of months he felt better accepted in his class, with a sense of belongingness that he enjoyed very much. Later he stopped his day patient routine without any serious upsurge of suicidal impulses.

Comments:

1. Psychiatric clients and, in my experience, especially near-'psychotic' clients, make all sorts of requests of their therapists. Time and again I have had the experience that therapy in effect comes to a halt and clients get worse if the therapist makes decisions with respect to these requests that they do not feel wholly comfortable with. Near-psychotic clients are very sensitive to therapist incongruence and the therapist not being fully present with them. They seem to become more helpless under the burden of feelings of anxiety about being rejected by the therapist and about being 'too much' for the therapist, and they will typically continue to become yet more helpless until the therapist regains their balance and realises that the client has actually become 'too much'. In this respect, the above example is very typical.

2. The example is also typical in the sense that it is the narcissistic wishes of the therapist, and their wishes to feel helpful, that contaminate the therapy process. Working with these clients is mostly a very long-term and inconspicuous affair: for long stretches of time nothing seems to happen; sometimes the client's condition deteriorates and, overall, progress is slow and inconspicuous, often in the form of three steps forward and two steps back. Reviewing the therapy over a long period, the therapist can notice progress in details in the quality of contact with the client and in the level of the client's experiential process in sessions, but other observers, possibly even the client him- or herself, often ignore this kind of gradual progress for a very long time. The work of the psychotherapist mostly goes unnoticed, and it is therefore important that the therapist is not burdened by pressing narcissistic wishes or wishes to feel immediately helpful. These

wishes of the therapist must be satisfied in other areas of work, which is why working exclusively with psychiatric clients in long-term therapy is rarely a good idea.

3. Furthermore, this example illustrates a typical core conflict for many psychiatric clients: the dependence/independence conflict. Many psychiatric clients have never experienced the possibility of being safe in a dependency relationship with significant others. For myriad reasons, they have developed a counter-dependent self-concept, giving up and denying or distorting wishes for dependency too early or too abruptly. They typically feel the stigma attached to being a psychiatric patient very clearly and very painfully and they will sometimes undertake very unrealistic actions in their struggle to become independent of the psychiatric system – the sooner the better. Some of these clients might have a very difficult process to go through in coming to accept some continuing dependency (as in, for example, taking up sheltered living facilities) before they can slowly develop in the direction of true independence. With the stress put on promoting independence and autonomy in the general theory of client-centred therapy, this process can be hard on the therapist too, and they can easily feel a failure in such circumstances.

4. In addition, the example illustrates the importance of distinguishing clearly between understanding and accepting a client's wishes for dependency on the one hand, and accommodating or satisfying them on the other. Most psychiatric clients typically receive several psychiatric services, not only psychotherapy. Many psychiatric services are geared to accommodate or satisfy client wishes for protection and dependency, but if psychotherapy becomes one of these it loses its *raison d'être*. Furthermore, realistically, the therapist cannot offer the protection of, say, hospitalisation, sheltered living facilities, sheltered educational facilities or visits by community psychiatric nurses etc. In the example, the risk of the client taking their life increased the longer the therapist colluded with the client's counter-dependent self-concept, because this did not meet the client's need for protection, dependency and care. This only happened when he was admitted to hospital as a day patient.

The example also illustrates the importance of good professional consultation or supervision. Time and again the therapist will want a place of their own where they feel safe to explore troubling, unclear feelings about limits in their relationship with a client. No therapist, however competent or experienced, can avoid getting into situations where they feel uncomfortable with their client, and with the 'difficult-edge' clients in any setting, the relevance of consultation or supervision is even more obvious.

5. When clients make requests of me like this I usually tell them that I would feel uncomfortable accommodating them. I explain that whether realistic or not, I would feel anxious and overburdened because I would feel responsible for their protection and, further, that I would not feel comfortable about the possibility of having other appointments disturbed. I am careful to take the full responsibility for my refusal by stating it clearly in personal terms, from my own frame of reference, and by expressing my regret that I am unable to accommodate them. Most importantly, I do not question the wisdom of the client's request by referring to what might or might not (from my frame of reference) be helpful to the client; I am not an expert on the client, but I am an expert on myself. This, and responding empathically to the client's experiences of these issues, leads of course to the client finding other ways to resolve their dilemma. Sometimes they find that their need for protection has disappeared or diminished by discussing it. Sometimes I agree to prolong a session to give us more time for this discussion, or I arrange an extra session as soon as possible. Sometimes we agree on a few telephone contacts at specified times that suit my schedule, or we agree to meet more frequently. Sometimes the client finds that they need more help and protection than I can satisfy, or help of a kind that I cannot provide. If I have been sufficiently comfortable with my own limits and at the same time sufficiently accepting of and empathic towards the client's wishes for protection, they might then change their request for something from me to a fruitful consideration of other means of protection, ranging from hospitalisation to, for example, a weekend at their grandparents', or a consultation with a psychiatrist to discuss medication.

With respect to limit setting, therapists are often concerned about negative consequences of limit setting for the client, themselves and the therapeutic relationship. Will the client lose trust in the therapist? Will the client feel judged, hurt, rejected? Will they become submissive, violent, reject the therapist and the therapy? Therapists can imagine all sorts of catastrophic consequences, including that the client will take their own life. This is understandable since there is really no way to predict the effect on the client of setting a limit. It may be helpful to look back over the relationship and other experiences with limit setting with that client, or to consult with somebody who knows the client, if that is possible within the boundaries of confidentiality and other ethical considerations. And, of course, supervision/consultation may be helpful to gain a more realistic perspective, as illustrated in the example above.

With respect to the risk that the client will leave the therapy as a consequence of the therapist setting limits, Rogers (1942: 99) wrote that he found it 'highly unlikely' that this would happen, but if it did, it would be 'more constructive than continuing it on a false basis'.

But it does happen. I was seeing a client who asked me how I preferred to have sex with my husband. This was in the context of his wish for more reciprocal disclosures of intimate experiences between us. While I accepted and empathised with his wish for reciprocity, I also told him I could not answer his question; it wouldn't feel right for me to do so. He stood up and said that he would not disclose all about himself if I were not willing to do the same, and then he left, slamming the door behind him. Reflecting on the experience afterwards, I ended up thinking that he chose very wisely: I could never become the therapist he apparently wanted and could never offer the friendship relationship with him that he apparently desired. Had I answered his question he might have stayed but we would surely then have been continuing on a false basis – as Rogers put it – since sooner or later I would have had to apologise to him for answering a question I felt I should not have answered, and to tell him that I would be more careful not to do so in the future. Sometimes it may be well to remember that therapists can help most potential clients but they cannot help them all, and that leaving with more of a bang rather than a whimper might actually be a step forward for a client.

In the midst of imagining these negative consequences for the client, it is easy to forget that, if the therapist does not respect their own limits, their capacity for experiencing acceptance and empathic understanding of the client will diminish; they will most likely get into some form of saviour/persecutor/victim triangle; and this will certainly harm the relationship with the client.

Peter, in the example above, did sense that I felt burdened by his phone calls and lost some of his sense of safety in the relationship. This sensitivity to any other than fleeting instances of therapist failures to respect their own limits is probably characteristic of most clients in most settings. Finely tuned antennae are characteristic of clients, particularly in relation to those perceived to be in positions of authority, and in the end most clients will resent the therapist who allows them to lean on illusions about their strengths.

Thus, when therapists do not respect their own limits, they will probably feel increasingly uncomfortable in some way or other – typically by feeling overburdened – and clients will sense this. Something very important is happening in the relationship, something that cannot be spoken about until the therapist breaks the silence and brings up the subject. Clients rarely bring it up, because they also feel in need of what the therapist offers as a result of exceeding their limits and perhaps also because they correctly feel that it is not their job or even that it is nothing to do with them. On one occasion, however, a client to whom I had agreed to offer a late evening session brought it up 10 minutes into the session: 'Lisbeth, you seem too tired. I'm sorry I asked for a session so late, I'll leave you so you can get off work and go home.' I could only agree that she was right, apologise for having accommodated her request when I knew I might feel too tired, and thank her for her sensitivity and consideration. I went home feeling rather ashamed of myself because, in the end, I was the one who had burdened her with coming to my office in vain.

We talked about this more in the next session and the client gave many examples of her own habit of exceeding her limits, of having difficulty saying 'no' to others, and described her feelings of anxiety when she saw me having the same difficulty. It had reduced her hope that it would be possible for her to state her limits to others better, and that they would be respected. I had been a bad model for her and it took time to repair our relationship in this respect and for her to come to trust my ability to respect my own limits again. This example can probably be generalised into stating that when a therapist models respect for their own limits it can be therapeutic for the many clients who get into problems because they find it hard to say 'no'.

Some common limit-setting issues

Limits with respect to suicidal behaviour

Suicidal behaviour, which is frequent among more fragile clients, ranks high among behaviours that especially challenge most therapists' limits.[2]

---

2. PCCS Books has kindly permitted me to take the following section about suicidal risk, in an adapted version, from my book *The Client-Centred Therapist in Psychiatric Contexts* (Sommerbeck, 2003: 61–67)

The person-centred therapist will probably find the issue of the prevention of suicide more problematic than psychotherapists from other orientations and other mental health professionals. Many feel that the client is best able to make the best decisions for themselves, including the decision to end their own life, and the client's thoughts about suicide should therefore not be interfered with or judged. Person-centred theory tells us that thoughts of suicide express the client's actualisation of his or her most constructive potential at that moment, and the core conditions of empathy, conconditional positive regard and congruence will release the client's own potential to consider all the possibilities, including possibilities other than suicide.

Nevertheless, when the risk of a client actually taking their life seems urgent, person-centred therapists often find themselves in a dilemma: do they intervene in the moment in an effort to prevent the suicide or do they trust that the core conditions will create a relationship that has a better chance of preventing the client from actually taking their own life when he or she has left the session? One way or other, whether for personal and/or legal reasons, the therapist will almost certainly want to prevent their client from actually ending their own life. The well-known, somewhat ridiculing joke about Rogers looking acceptingly at a client jumping out of the 13th floor window *is* just that – a joke.

In my own experience of working in a psychiatric hospital, when a depressed client disclosed acute suicidal ideation in a session with me, and I knew my colleagues were unaware of this, I found myself in dire conflict, with thoughts in all directions whirling around in my head. If I kept this information to myself, there would be no risk of my client being forcibly detained or treated against their will – an outcome which would have been antithetical to the philosophy and values of person-centred therapy. On the other hand, it seemed obvious that I should tell, because suicidal people often come to think and feel differently quite quickly, and by informing my psychiatric colleagues I would be preventing a tragic accident. While I trusted the facilitative potential of the core conditions, I dared not trust that they would achieve such major changes overnight.

When I decided to pass on information that my client *was* suicidal, I did so in opposition to what I most deeply wished to be able to do: namely, to trust the core conditions to facilitate the most constructive change possible in this client, as I had done with all other clients. I experienced myself as saying 'Yes, but ...' to the essence of person-centred therapy.

But other concerns also played a part. As a professional in a psychiatric institution, I was supposed to pass on this kind of information to the relevant team leaders and clinical director; not doing so would be a breach of my contract with my employer, and I did not want to jeopardise my position. Later I will explain why this kind of interference became an increasingly rare event in my practice, but first I will describe an example where I *did* interfere with my client's process, thereby placing myself in a position far removed from my values as a person-centred therapist – that of being the expert on what would be best for the client.

This was a client diagnosed with psychotic depression who in her first two sessions talked about her view of herself as a destructive person, guilty of much evil. For example, she believed she was responsible for the atrocities that took place during the civil wars in former Yugoslavia – she was convinced she would be caught and put on trial in The Hague and convicted for her crimes. She was also convinced that sooner or later the ward staff would become aware of her true evil nature and deliver her over to the International Court of Justice, even though they repeatedly assured her they would not. A tiny grain of truth in all this seemed to be that she did not support her son's wish to join the Danish military peacekeeping force in Yugoslavia. Apart from that, she was evidently delusional when her beliefs were looked at from any frame of reference except her own. This did not make any difference to my efforts to understand her empathically in my two first sessions with her.

In her third session she said that she was having thoughts of suicide as a way to avoid the humiliating trial in The Hague. She had also made concrete plans for how she might kill herself. She would walk to the nearby railway and throw herself in front of the train. She also said that making the driver of the train suffer by her action just showed how evil she was and always had been. She said that everything she did had *always* been destructive to others and now she could find no other sure way to kill herself than by making the driver of the train suffer. That, she said, was just the way she was. During the session she turned this over and over and came to a point where she said that she did want to kill herself in a foolproof way but she was plagued by the thought of the train driver feeling responsible for killing her. At the end of the session she said that she had started to feel a little better, a little relieved, during sessions with me and that this also happened when she talked to her two primary nurses. However, when these talks ended, she felt just as despairing as before, or even worse. Nevertheless her talks with the nurses and me provided little rays of light in her night-time of darkness.

After this session I had some thinking to do. I knew this client had not talked about suicide before and my evaluation was that her suicidal thinking was grounded in temporary, reversible psychotic ideation. She was typically a client whom the psychiatric system would be expected to keep safe from suicide. However, she had until that time been delusional in a quiet, non-destructive way, so she was in an open ward and could easily go out for a stroll in the surrounding park and forest without anybody noticing, giving her ample opportunity to get to the railway tracks.

Should I pass on this information to the staff members of her ward? What would be the consequences of passing it on? What kind of coercive intervention would she be subjected to? And if I decided to pass it on, how should I do it?

I wondered about risks to the therapy process. Might she lose confidence in me? Particularly, might she lose confidence in my confidence in her? Might she feel betrayed by me? Might she feel that I had left her isolated in her hell? On the other hand, suicide would be the end of any therapy, which I would find quite tragic, especially in light of the very likely reversibility of her condition. In spite of her statement that she had started to feel a little relief through her relationships with me and her primary nurses, I felt I needed more time to be assured that my relationship with her was strong enough to 'hold' her (together with the nurses' relationship with her) – and I wouldn't get that time if she killed herself. And, of course, I also thought of the consequences for her husband and children, and – just as she did herself – for the train driver.

And what about the consequences for me? How would I feel if she took her own life and I hadn't told anyone I knew about her plans? One way or the other, I felt convinced that it would be a very painful experience. In addition, it would be a great relief to pass on this information, to share the burdensome feelings of worry, doubt and responsibility with my colleagues in the ward. I also felt that not telling would be a breach of my contract with the hospital, and I did not want to lose the trust of my colleagues and managers.

In the end I decided that the consequences of telling would be less negative than the consequences of not telling. But I made this decision with an uneasy feeling that I was betraying both the person-centred philosophy and my client by making myself the expert on her and by interfering in what might have been the best decision for her.

The consequence of my passing on the information about my client's suicidal plans was that she was not allowed outdoors on her own until her condition was deemed sufficiently improved. Later she described her mixed feelings about my passing on the information. She said she had half-expected me to do it, knowing that in principle all staff, including me, had to feel free to share information about patients that they deemed it necessary to share. She felt relieved to have had the decision taken off her shoulders, but she also missed the feeling of security it gave her to know that she could end her pain by killing herself. She also expressed feeling shocked at the thought that she might have lost her life as a result of thinking so unrealistically. On the other hand, she thought it most likely that she would not have tried to kill herself – she felt a little hope that things would get better – so she was also somewhat disappointed that I didn't have enough confidence in her to believe that she would not do it. However, she said she understood why I had taken this action (she'd have done the same had she been in my shoes) and so she felt forgiving towards me.

All this was expressed in normal person-centred dialogue in sessions when her depression had lifted substantially.

It is, perhaps, noteworthy that I did not discuss my decisions to pass on information about their suicidal plans with my clients. I notified them, sometimes before, sometimes after the event, that I had shared the information. The decision was not up for discussion, although, of course, I explained the reasons for my decision if asked by the client. These decisions were made from my own perspective (and that of the hospital) and they were made knowing that any discussion with the client would not change my mind. I did not want to deceive the client into thinking that I might change my mind by discussing it, and I did not want to burden the client with my concerns: they were mine, not the client's. Furthermore, I did not want to risk getting into a relationship with the client where they might try to commit themselves to me by making promises about their future plans of action (promising not to take their own life, for example).

I felt that I protected my capacity to regain the experience of unconditional positive regard and empathic understanding of the client better by risking whatever reactions the client might have towards my unilateral decision. I very much wanted to welcome these reactions, as soon as possible, with unconditionally acceptant empathic understanding. This way of doing things, however, is normally not considered good practice. Normally therapists are expected to inform clients beforehand and invite questions and discussions. I have found that what is considered good professional practice does not always coincide with what I consider to be optimal client-centred practice. Whether to follow external judgments of good practice or one's own judgment of good practice can be a serious dilemma for therapists. Therefore, any client-centred therapist working in a context like psychiatry, where they often encounter suicidal clients, has to find his or her own position concerning the issue of suicide. Rogers (1951: 48) had the following to say:

> Does the counselor have the right, professionally or morally, to permit a client seriously to consider ... suicide as a way out, without making a positive effort to prevent this choice? Is it a part of our general social responsibility that we may not tolerate such thinking or such action on the part of another? These are deep issues, which strike to the very core of therapy. They are not issues which one person can decide for another. Different therapeutic orientations have acted upon different hypotheses. All that one person can do is to describe his own experience and the evidence which grows out of that experience.

Responding to the implicit question in this quotation, my own experience has been that, over the years, as my confidence in my competence as a therapist grew, decisions to disclose my clients' suicidal ideation and intentions to others became more rare. Yet only one of my clients has taken their own life, in over 35 years of working as a psychotherapist in a psychiatric context, where suicides are quite frequent. I learned that when a client discloses plans to end their own life they are still one or more crucial steps away from actually doing so. I also learned to become more trusting of that flicker of hope implicit in the client actually being there with me, and in the client's feeling less abandoned and isolated as a result of my willingness to keep listening and try to understand their suicidal ideation. Finally, and maybe most important, I became more convinced that the best precautionary measure I, as a person-centred therapist, could take with respect to suicidal risk was to remain the client's person-centred therapist, and nothing else.

But, as Rogers says, the therapist has to find their own answers with respect to their suicidal clients, perhaps even on an individual case-by-case basis. What I have written above worked for me, but may not work for others.

Limits with respect to violent behaviour

In order to practise therapy at all, it is of course exceedingly important, if not essential, that therapists are not afraid of their clients. In many settings this may not be much of an issue, but in some settings it certainly is, and therapists must find ways to feel secure with every client. It is their job, not the job of the client. In a psychiatric hospital, the risk of violent behaviour was an issue I had to take care of, particularly when working with clients from the locked ward. I learned this lesson the hard way when I was once exposed to violent behaviour from a client and handled the situation badly. After that episode, I developed some safety routines for myself.

First, I always made sure with all my clients that I would sit nearest to the door of my office. I would do this by placing my shawl on the chair where I usually sat (and, incidentally, I actually concentrated less well when I did not sit in that chair). Second, I decided I would leave the room immediately if I felt threatened by a client's aggressive behaviour. I would not stop to speculate, and even less to negotiate, as in any case I could not work properly if I felt scared and that I needed to get away. I would not ask the client to behave differently or to leave – I would not have expectations of the client, with the risk of experiencing negative regard for the client if he or she did not live up to my expectations. The responsibility to feel properly protected was purely my own. I would not ask the rain to stop because I was not properly dressed. Instead, I would get out of the rain to put on some protective clothes, which in this case meant asking a staff member from the client's ward to come back with me to my office to escort the client to their ward.

I felt very secure with all clients with this plan, which staff had agreed to, and I only once needed to act on the first part of it. In an outburst of anger a client turned over a little lamp on the table next to him. I felt frightened and immediately rose and went to the door, whereupon the client apologised and said that nothing like that would happen again. Knowing the client, I was reassured by his promise and sat down, and we continued the session. I suspect, but can of course not know, that my firm resolution to get out of the way of what I experienced as threatening behaviour had a positive effect in this case, and perhaps also in others; it was almost as if my confidence in my capacity to protect myself made threatening behaviour seem outlandish.

Other therapists' limits in situations like the one described above may be very different. Carl Adams (2012), for example, is very competent in physical self-defence, and teaches such techniques to other therapists. It is very likely that he and his students feel so secure with their competence – very different from the self-defence routine I developed –that it also prevents violence from their clients, who are young people from the streets, many with drug problems. As Jin Wu wrote in the e-mail discussion I reported earlier (p. 29): 'The client-centred therapist checks with themselves to see if honoring a client's request would compromise their ability to provide the conditions, so such limits vary a great deal from therapist to therapist.' And in this sense one could also agree with Dorothy Morgan, from the same e-mail discussion, that 'limits and limit setting would fall within the category of genuineness', suggesting, as Jin Wu said, that they will vary a great deal from therapist to therapist.

With this understanding, therefore, the examples of limits and limit setting I have offered from my own practice are not meant as recommendations for other therapists to adopt. They are only meant as illustrations of the ways limit setting can become necessary in person-centred practice and are intended to inspire other therapists to take their own limits seriously, respect them, and ensure that they are respected by others. But, of course, we all have our own needs and ways of protecting our capacity to experience unconditional positive regard and empathic understanding of the client.

Idiosyncratic limits

Most therapists will have limits in how they respond to suicidal and violent behaviour, even if their ways of dealing with these limits vary widely. Other limits are more particular to individual therapists, and many will vary from moment to moment and situation to situation for the same therapist. For example, clients frequently ask for more time. This is a request most therapists are sometimes able to accommodate and sometimes not, depending on their own availability and other factors. Other limits tend to be closer to being set in stone, even if they are still part of a process and not absolute – and, actually, even stones change over time. For example, being a relatively reserved and private person is one of my idiosyncrasies, and I'd probably have responded in exactly the same way if anyone had asked me how I had sex with my husband or something equally intimate and private. My routine of self-protection against violent behaviour is also relatively set in stone, and can be regarded as idiosyncratic in the sense that it acknowledges that I am neither big and strong nor physically courageous. I needed a self-protection regime that ensured that I would not get into any kind of physical fight with anyone, let alone a client.

Here are a few other examples of my idiosyncratic limits, which I hope will inspire other therapists to become more aware and respectful of their own. I have discovered that I can see no more than two depressed clients in consecutive sessions. In the past, when I happened to have three, I felt somehow contaminated by the hopelessness of the previous two and found myself identifying with the hopelessness of the third about his or her prospects for the future. I resolved this by rescheduling one of these clients to another day of the week.

Another example is my sensitivity to bad smells. It is quite common for clients in psychiatric hospital to neglect their personal hygiene. With one such client, I couldn't concentrate properly so I always took care to have an air freshener in my office when I was scheduled to see him.

Many of my limits took me by surprise. For example, on one occasion I noticed that the floor in front of a new client's chair was strewn with mud from their shoes, and my thoughts turned from the client to the cleaning staff who would have to clean it up. The thought disturbed me so much that I asked my client for a break, got a vacuum cleaner and removed the mud. (Incidentally, the client never brought mud on their feet again!)

Having said that, I always tried to deal with my limits as inconspicuously as possible to minimise the disruption to the therapeutic process. My limits were my problem, not the client's. Mostly clients did not ask for any explanations. My seating arrangements and the air freshener in my office were never questioned. I never drew attention to them or the reasons for them. I find that clients do generally accept the therapist's limits, just as Rogers' client did not request any explanation for his refusal to have sexual intercourse with her and Rogers did not offer any explanation either (see p. 26).

Likewise, I did not offer a 'list' of my limits for negotiation with new clients, since I couldn't know which, if any, they'd challenge, and they might also come to challenge a hitherto-unknown limit of mine that I wasn't aware of – as in the case of the client with muddy shoes. Demarcating various limits in the first session seems unnecessarily formal – if I were challenged, the limits would emerge naturally in due course. The only 'limits' I found it necessary to agree with the client were at the end of the first session when we agreed when, where, and for how long we would meet next time – if indeed the client wanted there to be a next time. If that was the case, I also made an agreement with them that we would notify each other when we needed to cancel a session.

Contextual Limits

Protecting myself and clients from physical violence and suicidal behaviour was not something I was expected to do in isolation, unsupported. My employer expected it of me and of all other staff in the psychiatric hospital where I worked. Thus, in this instance, my own limits coincided with the limits of the context in which I worked.

But this was not always the case. Sometimes I needed to protect the client's therapeutic space by refusing to accommodate some requests and expectations that my employer or my colleagues had of me.

This kind of limit setting most frequently involved the non-directive and non-evaluative qualities of person-centred practice that differ markedly from the directive and evaluative practice in psychiatric, medical model settings in general. The same is also the case for person-centred therapists in other working contexts. The idea of the therapist not being an expert on the client is rarely found outside person-centred circles.

A personal history of being a non-expert on clients in an experts' setting[1]

I graduated as a psychologist in Copenhagen in 1974 and immediately found employment as a clinical psychologist in a small psychiatric hospital. I stayed there until 2005, when I moved to another psychiatric hospital. That change, as well as my retirement in 2011, had everything to do with the issue of not being an expert on clients. I'll clarify this statement later.

At university I had read Rogers' *Client-Centered Therapy* (1951) and I knew immediately that I wanted to practise this kind of therapy. I was therefore very lucky to start my career as a psychotherapist in psychiatry at a time when the anti-psychiatry movement, as formulated by, for example, Cooper (1967) and Szasz (1961, 1987), was having a profound influence on Danish psychiatry. Even though Danish

1. This is an edited version of a previously published article (Sommerbeck, 2012). I am grateful to Taylor & Francis for their kind permission to reprint it here.

psychiatry stayed fundamentally orientated towards the medical model, it became much more humanistic in its approach to clients.

Also at that time a variety of psychotherapies were founded and developed, and even though they might compete to be 'the best', none of them could really prove that they were, indeed, the best. Psychotherapy research that compared outcomes of various therapies had not yet come of age.

Therefore, in those days there was no demand for such things as quality control, accreditation, benchmarking, risk assessment, auditing, or 'evidence-based practice', and so on. Indeed, some of these terms didn't even exist. It was a golden age of freedom from control, and I was allowed to practise in any way I decided would be best for my clients, using my clinical judgment.

This did not mean that it was unproblematic to practise person-centred therapy in a psychiatric setting. My practice had to be carefully protected from all the directive expertise of the setting, which could otherwise sometimes inadvertently impinge on the therapy process. In the first section below I'll describe the guidelines and limits I developed to protect the person-centredness of the therapeutic space I offered clients.

In the 90s things started to change in Danish psychiatry. The era of the kinds of control I mentioned above had begun. These controls and requirements reached the hospital where I worked with full force in 2005 and were the reason I moved to another psychiatric hospital – a very small hospital on a remote Danish island, where the manager still succeeded in keeping controlling forces at arm's length. Eventually she could not continue doing that, and in 2008 she left. From that time on, I was required to combine my therapies with various kinds of more directive expert work with my clients.

I did find ways to circumvent much of this and in the second section I'll describe some of these ways. This second section will be much shorter than the previous section since I had much less experience with it and didn't record any dialogues from it.

These regulatory requirements kept increasing and left me with increasingly less joy in my work but then I was lucky again. In 2011 I reached the age when you can retire in Denmark without significant economic consequences. So, once again, I left a place of work because it had become too much of a struggle to uphold a reasonable (in my view) degree of person-centredness in my work. Nevertheless, I count myself lucky to have had a full career where I have been able to practise fairly 'pure' person-centred therapy – or classical client-centred therapy.

When the therapist is free to practise in a fully person-centred way

Even if the client-centred therapist is allowed full freedom to practise without being an expert on the client, he or she will probably find that it is a relatively lonely practice in an otherwise very directive setting of experts-on-clients. There may be other psychotherapy colleagues but they will, more likely than not, practise according to one of the more widespread, well-known and more expert-directed psychotherapeutic approaches such as, for example, psychodynamic therapy or cognitive behavioural therapy. The client-centred therapist will most likely find that, to the extent that their non-expert position is *permitted* in this setting of experts, it is not *well understood* or *appreciated*. After all, staff members in a medical model setting are educated to be experts on their clients; this is their professional *raison d'être*, and they naturally assume the same is the case for all other professionals in the setting. This means that, in spite of the freedom to practise person-centred therapy, the person-centred therapist will nevertheless often be expected by other professionals to be an expert on the client, and behave accordingly. Indeed being the expert on the client may well be seen to be good professional practice, and the client-centred therapist might feel under further pressure to comply.

It can therefore be very difficult for the client-centred therapist to navigate in this landscape of expertise-on-clients without themselves becoming experts on their clients. In the following paragraphs, I'll describe some of the difficulties and some of the ways to overcome these difficulties that have been fruitful, in my own experience.[2] The main point is to simultaneously protect the person-centredness of the therapy process and respect the therapist's 'contract' with the expert medical model.

First, the therapist has to consider refusing to accommodate

2. It is important that readers note that these are taken from my experience, and cannot be adopted in any and all professional situations. They are presented here as prompts for discussion and as tentative proposals. Readers will soon discover what is and is not possible in their own work setting. My message is to be active in pursuing ways to practise person-centred therapy effectively and comfortably within a medical model environment.

certain requests from the medical model staff that seem perfectly natural to them. The therapist may say 'no', for example, when they are asked in passing to just cast an eye on evaluating the client's condition in their next session. Staff members may want this evaluation to help them make all sorts of decisions; it is second nature for them, and part of their job, to make (diagnostic) evaluations when relating with clients; it is expected of them and they expect it of others. It can be difficult for non-informed staff members to understand and respect that the client-centred therapist can have no plans or intentions of any kind when they meet their clients.

The therapist can also be asked to talk certain things over with the client or deliver a message. Again, the person-centred therapist would consider refusing to accommodate these requests in order not to have any agenda for their session with the client other than empathically understanding the client from the client's own frame of reference. Jerold Bozarth (1990: 63) puts it well when he writes:

> The therapist goes with the client – goes at the client's
> pace – goes with the client in his/her own ways of
> thinking, of experiencing, of processing. The therapist
> cannot be up to other things, have other intentions,
> without violating the essence of client-centred therapy. To
> be up to other things – whatever they might be – is a 'yes
> but' reaction to the essence of the approach.

Second, the therapist must carefully consider whether or not to participate in meetings about their therapy clients if they think their participation might have negative consequences for the therapeutic process. The medical model setting ordinarily involves all sorts of collaborative meetings, and whether to participate or not is a delicate point and sometimes difficult for the therapist to decide: will their participation place them in the role of the powerfully influential expert on what is best for the client, either in the eyes of the client or in the eyes of others? Would participation be to the detriment of the therapy process? The therapist must, of course, be able to explain their decision, and respectful discussion can lead to better understanding of the person-centred therapist's position.

I was fortunate in my workplace to be able to only participate in these meetings if I knew I could take the position of facilitator for the participants with respect to their own process with the client. I refused to participate if I, as the client's psychotherapist and as an expert, was expected to tell my colleagues what was wrong with the client and what the best way was to 'fix' him or her. If this was the expectation, I deferred to one of the numerous experts-on-clients in the setting. Thus, my role in these meetings was similar to that of a person-centred group facilitator. In my experience, my participation in this role was much appreciated, and I also saw it as the best way for me to educate about – or rather demonstrate – the value of a person-centred approach.

The guiding principle in such situations is to do your best to avoid taking on the role of expert on what will be best for the client in any context.

Third, the therapist must be careful about sharing information on their therapy clients with the other professionals in the setting who are also engaged in helping the client – for example, the client's GP, psychiatrist, social worker, occupational therapist etc. The main point is not to say anything that others may inadvertently and unbeknownst to themselves use – with the best of intentions - in their relationship with the client in ways that may harm the therapy process. Imagine what would happen if another professional said to the client: 'I know from your therapist that…' As a rule of thumb, when in doubt, it is better to say too little than too much.

The therapist who is co-working with other professionals cannot, however, guarantee their client full confidentiality with respect to these professionals. This is inherent in the contract and the setting in which the therapist is working. For co-working to succeed, there can be no formal limits as to the information the professionals can share between them. This may seem to contradict the above statement about being careful with sharing information from the therapy with other professionals in order to protect the process of therapy. However, information of the kind that other staff members need to do their work very rarely surfaces in therapy sessions. Some clients would ask me about my criteria for passing on information about them to other staff members. I would tell them that I might pass on information that clients were suicidal or if they were taking other medication (or drugs), or taking it in ways other than that prescribed by their GP or psychiatrist.

In my experience these were the only two areas where I sometimes found it necessary, as a consequence of my contract with the medical model, to pass on information to other professionals with or without my client's agreement. Fortunately, these occasions were extremely rare. First, the other professionals usually knew about these things anyway. Second, clients generally know and expect that professionals, including the therapist, will talk to each other about them; that it is the obligation of professionals in the medical model to do what they can to prevent suicide among clients and that GPs and psychiatrists depend on information about the client's medicine and drug intake to monitor any psychopharmacological treatment. It is important to note, though, that the person-centred therapist does not always pass on this kind of information; the point is that the therapist must feel free to do so according to his or her own judgment.

However seldom it has occurred, I've found the decision to pass on information that my client is suicidal particularly hard to make because of the possibility of coercive treatment to prevent him or her from ending their life. I have often been in a real dilemma between the client-directed model of person-centred therapy and the expert-directed medical model on this issue. I have already discussed this in depth in relation to the example on pp. 39–42, which illustrates and expands on the issue of suicide and provides an equally good example here of the influence of contextual limits with respect to suicide on the person-centred therapist's practice.

Sometimes raising the issue of confidentiality and disclosure of information with the client can have repercussions for the relationship and therapeutic process – both positive and negative. It is not possible to plan a strategy for such events, other than to note that everything discussed in the session is potential grist to the mill as far as the therapeutic process is concerned.

To sum up about the issue of sharing information: the therapist does not share information from the therapy with other staff members if he or she thinks that this may have harmful consequences for the therapy process. On the other hand, they do not stay silent if they feel this to be against their own ethical standards and the safety of their job. Sacrificing either of these will *not* help the client. On the contrary, it leads to the vicious saviour/victim/persecutor triangle in the therapist's relationship with the client. Finally, other staff members very rarely need information from psychotherapy to do their own work, and the therapist very rarely needs information from other treatment modalities to do his or her work. Therefore, it is likely to be rare that there are truly good reasons for information to be shared between the therapist and other staff members.

Fourth, the therapist does not try to control the way other professionals treat his or her therapy clients. The therapist is aware that the client is in a medical model setting and is receiving other kinds of help apart from psychotherapy, and offers the professionals in the medical model the same respect that he or she expects and hopes for from them.

However, the person-centred therapist may sometimes feel that the professionals of the expert-on-the-client medical model treat their client with little respect and understanding and they can feel tempted to try to protect the client by seeking to change and control what these other professionals do. This is a mistake. First, it amounts to identification with the client; clients must, after all, find their own ways of dealing with their world and protecting themselves in it, including the world of the medical model. (Would the therapist contact the client's mother, for example, to try to influence her to treat the client with more respect and understanding?) Second, what seems disrespectful or insensitive to the therapist may not seem so to the client. Third, trying to change the ways of others with their client implies that the therapist regards him/herself as an expert on what is best for the client, which is quite antithetical to person-centred theory and risks ruining the therapy process. Protecting the client and protecting the therapy process are two very different, sometimes even mutually exclusive, endeavours. My work with Peter (pp. 32–55) was an example of this.

Below follows an example that illustrates some of the points of this section, which I offer for discussion.

Marion was 30 years old, married, with a five-year-old son. She had been admitted to hospital on her own initiative because of frequent psychotic episodes where she heard voices ordering her to stab, variously, her husband, her son and herself to death. She was treated with medication, which she felt helped her, and she had started in psychotherapy. She had also started going home for the weekends, but this occasioned an upsurge in her symptoms. In the therapy she hesitatingly began to express very negative feelings towards her husband. This was a change from the first sessions, where she mostly talked about her voices and her fear of giving in to them. In the ward, too, staff-members had an impression of problems at home: because of the decline in her condition after weekends, because her husband never visited her, and because she tried to foreshorten her weekend passes, telling her primary nurse that she was a burden on her husband when she was at home. He had to take care to keep knives locked away from her; he had to do all the cooking and other work in the kitchen because it involved the use of knives; and he couldn't leave her alone.

Her condition and treatment were discussed in the regular, weekly staff conference, and the following dialogue evolved between the chief psychiatrist of the ward (CP) and the therapist (T):

CP: I really think we can't get further in the treatment of Marion without some sort of couples therapy. As it is now, I can't imagine her out of hospital in the foreseeable future, and we have many patients on the waiting list. (Turning to T): What about you having some couples sessions with Marion and her husband?

T: I'll gladly do that, if Marion wants me to.

CP: OK, then you talk with her about that and we can see how it progresses.

T: Oh, no, wait a minute. I'll not introduce this idea or any other to her. You know I only work with issues that she brings up herself.

CP: (Smiling) Sorry, I forgot for a minute that you have this peculiarity. Then I'll propose it to her and suggest that she brings it up with you, if that is OK with you?

T: Sure, that's fine with me.

Two days later Marion (M) comes for her ordinary session and immediately brings up the subject of couples sessions.

M: CP said to me that it would be a good idea if I brought Douglas along to some talks with you.

T: Uhm, hmm... (a short silence)

M: But I don't know...

T: You are not sure it would be such a good idea?

M: No... I know I've told you that there are some things about Douglas that make me furious sometimes, but he also helps me a lot, and... I don't know... I don't feel like sitting here telling him about these things. I am sure it would make him feel bad, and I'd understand that. I'd feel bad if he gave me a scolding in front of a stranger, too.

T: You feel sort of disloyal at the thought of bringing him here for a scolding. He doesn't deserve that because you also appreciate his helping you so much?

M: Yes, disloyal, and I'd also feel ashamed, as a coward. I should talk all these things over with him when we are by ourselves. It's just so difficult because he doesn't like to talk about that kind of thing.

Marion continues to discuss various aspects of her problems with her husband and decides that she will not bring her husband with her to a session. She prefers to try to find a way to have a talk with her husband at home about how she experiences their relationship. Then she turns to the therapist:

M: Will you tell CP that I won't bring Douglas in, explain it to him?

T: For some reason you'd rather have me do it than do it yourself?

M: Yes, I'm afraid he'll be annoyed with me because I won't bring Douglas in, but I'm sure he'd respect it if you told him.

T: Takes courage to say no to CP?

M: It sure does – I'm afraid he'll dismiss me from hospital soon if I don't accept his proposal, so will you tell him?

T: You think that if I tell him, he won't dismiss you so soon?

M: Yes... Oh, why should that make a difference... It's just that sometimes it is a little difficult to talk with CP. He always seems to be in a hurry, a little impatient, and that makes me nervous. So I'd appreciate it if you would talk with him?

T: You tend to feel nervous with CP, because you feel pressured when he seems to be in a hurry, and you'd prefer to avoid that by having me talk with him?

M: Yes, but... Well, I ought to do it myself. I'll talk with him myself.

T: You feel an obligation to do it yourself?

M: (Laughing) Yes, and I'm also a little annoyed with you,

because I think you won't do it, but then I also just thought that this is the kind of situation I always try to avoid, saying no to others, and particularly to authorities, and it doesn't do me any good in the long run.

Marion spent the rest of the session coming to terms with her annoyance with me and preparing how best to tell CP about her decision not to have couples sessions. She was transferred to day patient status two weeks later and after a month or so as a day patient she was discharged from hospital altogether. She continued with the psychotherapy as an outpatient, and for a while she also continued to see CP about her medication, until this aspect of her treatment was transferred to her GP. Her psychotic symptoms had almost disappeared, she had managed to engage her husband in talks about their relationship, and generally things were going much better at home. In the final phases of therapy she no longer heard any voices and the predominant theme was her fear of being alone. When she overcame that fear, she ended therapy after little less than three years. At that time her GP had also agreed with her to end the medication. We never heard from her again.

Comments:

1. The dialogue from the staff conference is typical of the therapist's work to avoid getting into situations with their clients where they will be the expert. The therapist avoids becoming an advocate and messenger from the medical model professionals to their client. Such situations occur in countless variations and disguises.

2. When the chief psychiatrist mentions the possibility of couples therapy sessions during the staff conference, the therapist has a hunch, from her sessions with the client, that the client will not like this idea. The therapist, though, sees no point in speaking about this hunch, because she also wants to avoid acting as an advocate and messenger from the client to the medical model professionals. The therapist does not try to influence the psychiatrist, respecting that the psychiatrist will make the most constructive choice possible for him from his frame of reference, which, among other things, also includes balancing his resources as fairly as possible between hospitalised patients and patients on the waiting list.

3. The client's process in the therapy hopefully illustrates how harmful it would have been if the therapist had either suggested couples sessions to the client (on behalf of her medical model colleagues), or suggested to the psychiatrist that couples sessions might not be beneficial (on behalf of the client).

4. Clients in medical model settings often ask the therapist to talk on their behalf to other professionals in the setting. When I answered this question (in the example above, I did not), I normally just explained that I couldn't do this because it was important for me not to confuse my particular relationship with them with other things. This mostly sufficed, and I would then try to empathically understand the client's reaction to my refusal to accommodate their request. Of course my knowledge that clients had other helpers in addition to me in the psychiatric system (social workers, primary nurses etc) made it easier for me to insist on remaining within a purely psychotherapeutic relationship with the client. If I had been in, say, private practice, I can imagine situations where I would have accepted the role of advocate for the client – for example in relation to benefits entitlements or employment support – because I knew they'd listen more respectfully to me than to the client; trust my word for what the client needed better than the client's own word; and I'd be more concerned about the client getting this kind of help than about the consequences to our therapeutic relationship. (See the chapter about extra-therapeutic relationships.)

5. The psychiatrist hinting at the 'peculiarity' of the therapist is probably a rather more common occurrence for a person-centred therapist than for therapists from other orientations, who would be more willing to introduce issues from outside their own frame in their sessions with clients. The person-centred therapist's dedication to safeguard the client's freedom and autonomy in the therapy process, and the importance this therapist attaches to the locus of initiative resting firmly with the client in their relationship, are rarely fully understood outside person-centred circles. It can therefore seem a superfluous and roundabout procedure to other professionals when they (like CP, in the example) must themselves propose to the client that they talk something over with the therapist that the therapist is perfectly willing to discuss with the client in the first place.

The essence of the issues that have been dealt with in this section can be summed up as follows:

- The therapy progresses best in parallel, not integrated, with the medical model treatments; it is preferable to keep these two worlds separated by a clear boundary.
- There is very little need to share information with others about a client if this is only done for truly good reasons.
- The therapist takes care in their relationship with the client not to identify with, or become the advocate or messenger of, the medical model.
- When working in an agency setting, the therapist takes care in their relationship with other professionals not to identify with, or become the advocate for, or messenger of the client.

Dave Mearns (1994: 53–56) has stressed the importance of the therapist being 'beside' the client, not 'on the side of' the client. This is, to me, a very important point to stress. At the same time, it is equally important to be 'beside' but not 'on the side of' the agency, or any other context or position.

All this is much easier said than done. The therapist can sometimes feel quite split between the person-centred world of their therapy sessions and the world of experts-on-clients outside the therapy sessions. These two worlds can seem mutually exclusive or contradictory, and the temptation to get into discussions about which world is the better for the client can be great. It is important that the therapist does not fall for this temptation in their daily work with individual clients and the individual professionals who are also engaged in helping the client and, just like the therapist, are truly doing the best they can. Falling for this temptation amounts to making themselves an expert on individual clients and risks making the client a hostage in a war between the person-centred model and the medical model. Discussions about which world is the better for clients should take place only in relation to clients in general, i.e. in more generalised, theoretical discussions, not in relation to individual clients.

In this respect it can be helpful for the therapist to conceptualise the two worlds as complementary instead of contradictory, in the same way that physicists speak of complementarity when discussing the wave/particle duality of, say, the electron. In one experimental set-up the electron *is* a particle, in another it *is* a wave. Thus, whether the electron is an electron or a wave depends on the physicist's choice of viewpoint. In the same way, whether the client is a unique being and thus an unknown being on whom it is impossible to be an expert, or whether the client is in some most likely diagnostic way an 'average' being and thus a known being on whom it is possible to be an expert, depends on the professional's choice of viewpoint. Unique or average? Clients can benefit from both viewpoints, but the two positions cannot be held simultaneously. Of course, in the expert-on-the-client medical model setting, it is mostly the person-centred therapist, exclusively, who chooses the standpoint that the client *is* a unique being.

Assessing and diagnosing

Rogers offers two objections to diagnosis from a person-centred perspective:

> In the first place, the very process of psychological diagnosis places the locus of evaluation so definitely in the expert that it may increase any dependent tendencies in the client, and cause him to feel that the responsibility for understanding and improving his situation lies in the hands of another... When the locus of evaluation is seen as residing in the expert, it would appear that the long-range social implications are in the direction of the social control of the many by the few. (Rogers, 1951: 223–24)

In this way, any kind of psychological diagnosis raises the client's expectations of the diagnostician engaging in some authoritative expert practice to help the client, based on their diagnosis, akin to a prescription. One could ask, 'Why else would the expert want the diagnosis?' From this perspective assessing and diagnosing are hard, if not impossible, to reconcile with *not* being an expert on the client. Some person-centred therapists, however, do value assessment, and argue that it is necessary (Sachse, 2004; Speierer, 1990; Swildens, 2004) to offer clients optimal therapy. Specifically with reference to the Counselling for Depression (CfD) therapy offered through England's IAPT (Improving Access to Psychological Treatment) programme, Sanders writes (Sanders & Hill, 2014: 125–26):

> So, in psychological therapy services associated with counselling for depression, assessment involves getting

> a sense of the problem from the client's own point of
> view, looking at the history and development of the
> problem(s), getting a sense of the client's resilience and
> vulnerabilities and collaboratively agreeing a course
> of therapy ... Our intention is to lay the foundation for
> assessment to be creatively developed and implemented
> by CfD practitioners within their local service framework.

Even one of the most ardent advocates of the non-directive attitude in person-centred therapy, Jerold Bozarth (1988: 128–31), expands on three circumstances where person-centred therapists could engage in assessment by the use of measures, as follows:

- The client requests assessment or the use of measures.
- The agency or professional setting may require assessment.
- The client and therapist might have to make a decision regarding future treatment suggested by such mediators of therapeutic possibilities as agency protocols, funding or the law. Assessment or diagnostic tools might afford an 'objective' view which could inform the client's and therapist's decision.

During the last years of my career, the trend towards increased control and rationalisation in the name of improvement that has become characteristic of health systems all over the Western world naturally reached Denmark as well. The first consequence for my work was a request from my new manager to participate in some (to me, but not necessarily to others (see above)) non-person-centred practices with my clients: regular (around once-a-month) diagnostic interviewing, evaluation of progress and suicide risk assessment, all carried out by me personally, using questionnaires and checklists. The results were to be noted in the client's report and were also sometimes sent to external authorities on which the client depended for various kinds of support, mostly financial.

Although I only used these practices for about three years before I retired, I did develop some guidelines for carrying them out so they did not seriously 'stain' the person-centred attitude with which I wanted to meet clients.

One guideline I developed for myself was to separate these practices in time and place from the therapy sessions. I drew a boundary between the two and regarded the assessments as extra-therapeutic activities. I scheduled an extra one or two hours a month or so to complete the processes with each of my clients, late in the afternoon when I could be sure to find an empty office in the hospital so I did not have to use my own.

Most clients fully understood and accepted this arrangement and were grateful that I didn't take time from their therapy sessions to do all this assessment. However a few outpatients, particularly those who lived at quite a distance from the hospital, didn't want to come in other than for the therapy sessions. With these very few clients I asked their permission to come to their home instead, acknowledging that our job was, indeed, requested by the setting, not by the client. This was accepted by all.

A serious drawback of this arrangement was, of course, the extra workload on me. I tried to make up for it by reducing my participation in other meetings but this was unacceptable to my colleagues and manager. In the end I had to reduce the number of clients that I could see in therapy. That was more acceptable to the hospital authorities, which to me demonstrated the decreased valuing of psychotherapy (perhaps with the exception of cognitive behavioural therapy) in psychiatric settings in recent years. It was not nearly as acceptable to me – I regretted that fewer clients now received an offer of psychotherapy. My manager naturally regretted this as well, which (further) strained our relationship, although she did not go so far as to order me to change my decision to use extra time on assessment procedures – a practice that was particular to me, and not shared by any other professional in the setting.

I also developed the practice of carefully explaining to clients that I was required to do these assessments by the setting (i.e. my manager) and that the assessments had nothing to do with our therapy relationship; that I was not assessing them in my role as their therapist but in my role as one professional among many others in the hospital who might just as well have made these assessments with them. I also told them that they might find they'd benefit from the assessments in their contacts with other professionals in the setting, although there was a risk that the reverse might also be true: that the assessments might lead to some intervention that they'd find unhelpful rather than helpful. This risk was, however, much diminished by my efforts to ensure the clients had the last word in the assessment.

In short, I told them that assessments would be inconsequential for our therapy work but that they were of course welcome to bring experiences from the assessments into the therapy sessions, just as with any other of their experiences. And this sometimes did happen, particularly in the first therapy session after the assessment session.

I also decided to let the client have the last word. I took great care that the clients recognised themselves in the results of the assessments – that they considered results to be an accurate statement of their own experience of suicidal risk, progress (or the reverse) and diagnosis. With respect to the latter, we went through the list of diagnoses and used the one that the client thought best matched their experience of their problems and/or symptoms. Sometimes this meant that we had to make corrections to the questionnaire so it came out with the desired result. I also let the client be the final judge as to what I'd write in their report.

In this way the final assessment was a collaboration between me and my client, much more than it was an assessment by an expert-on-the-client professional. Actually, it was mostly the clients' assessment of themselves. But this was, of course, not the intention and with some clients I ended up in a dilemma between my wish to respect my person-centred therapy process with the client and my wish to respect my contract with my employer, not unlike the dilemma with regard to suicidal clients that I described above. For example, a few times in the three years I used these assessments it happened that a questionnaire turned out positive on delusional ideation and/or hallucination, resulting in a diagnosis of psychosis, which the client disputed because they were convinced of the reality of their experiences. In these cases, except for two, the client agreed that we would write their version of their reality alongside mine in the report, and it did not harm the therapy process in the long run. But, much to my despair, in two cases it did harm the therapy process lastingly, and both these clients eventually ended the therapy.

All in all, though, I did manage to work to these guidelines to the satisfaction of all involved, including me. I also believe that quite a few of my clients fared better with my way of doing assessments than they would otherwise have done. And sometimes clients and I actually had fun doing the assessments together.

To end this section it may be worth noting again that what I have just described was *my* practice with assessments. As already noted there are person-centred practitioners who do not regard assessments as a sometimes-necessary evil and embrace them as benefiting the therapy. The practice of assessment in Counselling for Depression is a case in point (Sanders & Hill, 2014).

The end of being a non-expert on clients in an experts' setting

The pressure on my non-directive attitude increased when I was also asked to become case manager for my therapy clients and use 'evidence-based practice' with some of them.

Being a case manager meant that I had to make all kinds of decisions on behalf of my clients. Should they start in occupational therapy? Did they need help from a social worker? Could a hospitalised client go home for the weekend? Was the client well enough to become an outpatient? Should day-patient status be restricted or increased? Should the client see a psychiatrist about medication? And so on.

Previously, clients had discussed these issues with other professionals, mostly with their psychiatrist or primary nurse. Now they were supposed to discuss them with me, on their initiative or, even more, on mine, since I was supposed to monitor and direct their process in the setting. I had absolutely no hope of being able to protect a person-centred therapy process under these conditions. I was expected to become as directive and as much of an expert-on-the-client as the other professionals in the setting and this, as I saw it, in practice prevented me from working as a person-centred therapist. Around the same time an order was also issued that only cognitive behavioural therapy was to be practised with clients with diagnoses of mild to moderate depression, because it had been decided in the regional mental health directorate that this was the only evidence-based treatment for these clients. This decree was later withdrawn when the directorate became somewhat wiser about 'evidence-based practice'. Nevertheless, the request to be a case manager was more than enough to make me realise that my long career as a person-centred therapist in a medical model setting had come to an end. I had reached my ultimate limit. It was with a mixture of relief and sadness, but more the latter than the former, that I opted for retirement and sent in my resignation. But, of course, other person-centred practitioners may take up the challenge where I gave up, and find ways to be person-centred case managers, however much this sounds like a contradiction in terms.

Thus, this story does not have a happy ending. The therapist can only be as person-centred as the context permits.

I was more optimistic when I wrote *The Client-Centred Therapist in Psychiatric Contexts,* which also has a section about contextual limits (Sommerbeck, 2003). At that time I had been allowed many years of person-centred practice, and had almost come to believe that this was the universal and permanent state of affairs, to be expected as a given, not something to be particularly grateful for. It is only today that I realise how mistaken I was, how lucky I had been and how much gratitude I owe my previous managers.

I am therefore happy to have had the opportunity in the last section to correct my acontextual over-optimism in my 2003 book and to underline, instead, the context-dependency of every practitioner.

As the Stanford prison experiment demonstrated (Zimbardo, 2008), context can make brutes of us all – or, to paraphrase, 'experts-on-the-client'.

The insidious contagion of contextual rules

It is probably evident from my history in a psychiatric context, as described above, that I was *very* concerned about my limits with respect to the more or less unspoken rule that professionals are experts on their clients. This is not surprising, since not being an expert on clients is such an essential characteristic of person-centred therapy.

However, with the wisdom of hindsight, I can see that there were also implicit rules in that context that had an insidiously contagious effect on me, so that I failed to set limits with respect to them when it might have been appropriate. Even though all work settings implicitly or explicitly impose constraints, it is simply good professional practice to respectfully question them in the interests of better service to our clients, raising legitimate theoretical, ethical and practical questions along the way.

One limit that I rather unwittingly adopted was the limit of 50–60-minute sessions. The weekly schedule of all therapists in this context was built on sessions of a maximum of 60 minutes. Some clients were expected to use less time, and any time left over would be used for various kinds of desk work. It would have meant really hard work to reorganise this schedule to offer some of my clients sessions of more than 60 minutes. But I could have done it, and I didn't even think of it, even if I can see now, several years later, that some might have profited from longer sessions if I had been generally more flexible about this contextual 'rule'.

There was also the unspoken rule that sessions took place in the therapist's office. I was somewhat more aware of this rule and more flexible about it than I was about the 50–60-minute sessions. Occasionally I held sessions with clients in places other than my office. This happened mostly with clients I approached on my own initiative to try to relate to them in a pre-therapeutic mode. Mostly I approached them in their room, but I would also sometimes join someone on a bench in the park to smoke a cigarette with them, or walk with them to the grocer to buy a drink, and once to McDonalds to have a burger. And then there were clients who had their 'own' chair in the ward's living room, and the only place to approach them was there. However I stopped this latter practice after an event that was actually quite funny. I had made it a habit of joining a client – let's call him Alex – for around half an hour in the afternoon in the living room, where he always sat at the end of a sofa table, hardly ever speaking a word. Next to him sat another patient, John, and I would sit down on Alex's other side. Then something like the following conversation would take place:

Lisbeth: (to Alex) You are rolling cigarettes.

John: (to Lisbeth) Yes, Alex smokes a lot.

Lisbeth: (to Alex) John says that Alex smokes a lot.

[Alex is apparently oblivious to anything but rolling cigarettes.)]
John: (to Lisbeth) Alex doesn't talk much.

Lisbeth: (to Alex) John says that Alex doesn't talk much.

John: (to Lisbeth) He sits there all day, except when his mother visits – then he disappears.

Alex: I don't like her to come, so I go into the park.

Lisbeth: You don't like her to come and so you escape into the park.

Alex: Yes, she always just tells me what to do and what not to do – to stop smoking, to eat less, to exercise more…

Lisbeth: You don't want her to boss you around.

John: (to Lisbeth) He just rushes out when she is coming.

Lisbeth: (to Alex) John says you rush out from here when your mother is coming.

Alex: Yes, I run into the park and sit on a bench, but she just

>   runs after me and finds me – she is all over the place.
>
>   And so on.

Alex's primary nurse told me that Alex would speak more during these half-hour conversations than he did during the whole of the rest of the day. She also told me that John enjoyed the conversations and he would, a little in advance of the time when I usually arrived, remind Alex that 'our' therapist was due to come at any minute.

Alex, John and I were, however, not alone in the living room. Other clients spent a lot of time there and, because the ward was a rehabilitation ward for long-term clients of mixed communication skills, there were also clients there with much better communication skills than Alex. A woman among them was offered therapy with me by her primary nurse. She flatly refused, saying that she would not speak with a person who just repeated what she said. The primary nurse managed to persuade her to have a 'trial session' with me, explaining that I would of course relate in a different way with her than I did with Alex. In the end we had a fine course of therapy together, but this incident did make me wary about 'living-room sessions', and because I also had concerns about confidentiality I discontinued the practice. Instead I suggested to Alex that we could talk in his room, which he accepted if John could participate too. So we got permission from the staff for this, even though patients were normally forbidden to enter each other's rooms. There are limits on where therapy can be practised, as there are limits on appropriate times.

In my experience, however, many clients like Alex find it hard to communicate in face-to-face contact alone. The intimacy and privacy of that situation seems to make them feel uncomfortable and they prefer a more public setting, or some 'third' element – i.e. anything but them – that can capture the attention of both parties.

Limits on the number of sessions

Most person-centred therapists, dedicated to client self-determination as they are, would probably prefer the client to choose when to end the therapy. This may be possible for clients who pay for their own therapy. In recent years, however, it has become increasingly common for therapists to have the therapy paid for by some third party – the agency that they work for, an insurance company and the like. These third parties often put limits on the number of sessions they are willing to pay for. It is important, therefore, that person-centred therapists come to terms with any limits there may be on the length of therapy their clients can have, even if the therapist in most cases has the option of applying for (a limited number of) extra sessions if the stipulated number turns out to be insufficient. And avoiding the role of expert-on-the-client in relationship with the client, while being an expert-on-the-client in relationship with the third party, is of course important when making this kind of application, just as it is when making referrals (see Chapter 5 below).

Keith Tudor (2008) makes the following essential points in *Brief Person-Centred Therapies*. He describes two opposing attitudes to time limits that he has found among person-centred therapists: one that refuses to accept externally imposed time limits, most prominently exemplified by Dave Mearns, and one that accepts such limits as an unavoidable aspect of life, which is ultimately time limited by death. Most therapists, among them Tudor, probably accept time limits, and he stresses the importance of this acceptance being genuine rather than the therapist grudgingly submitting to the time limit and subtly communicating this to the client: 'We *only* have ten sessions.' In the latter case Tudor predicts a failure of therapy because neither therapist nor client really trusts the process, despite quite a lot of research, which he cites, demonstrating positive outcomes from brief therapy (Tudor, 2008, pp. 4–5).

Tudor refers to Maureen O'Hara, who points out that therapists facilitate the client's movement in the moment and that therefore there is no need to be concerned about time limits: clients will move or have moments of movement in whatever time frame is available. Notions like these and the research that supports them can help therapists hold the therapeutic space in time-limited therapy, rather than feeling under pressure and perhaps falling for the temptation to change their usual ways of working in the hope of speeding up the process. The challenge of brief therapy, says Tudor, is simply to be the best we can be in a shorter time: no more, no less. Interested readers can learn how John Shlien beautifully lives up to this in a case presentation of time-limited therapy (with excerpts of dialogue) included in Tudor's book (ibid: 85–102).

I have no experience of time-limited therapy. I like to think, however, that I would have worked like John Shlien if I had been asked to practise within a limited numbers of sessions. I like to think that I'd have related to the client with unconditionally accepting empathic understanding, just as I did with all my other clients. And, turning this point upside down, if I really thought there was something I could offer the client to speed up the process, apart from the core conditions, I'd actually consider it my duty to offer it to all my clients, not only those in brief therapy. There is no good reason why *any* therapy, time-limited or not, should last longer than necessary.

Limits as 'Time Out'

Generally, when a therapist needs to attend to his or her limits, whatever kind they may be, it can be regarded as their request for 'time out' from therapy. This is of course evident when the therapist brings up an issue of limits outside the therapy session, typically in supervision – and, as already noted, this issue is indeed often brought up in supervision. But bringing up the issue directly with the client can also be regarded as a therapist request for 'time out' from the therapy. As long as the therapist is attending to his or her limits, they are not attending to the client's frame of reference and is therefore not practising person-centred therapy, at least not in the classical understanding of the meaning (Frankel & Sommerbeck, 2007a). I have in earlier sections given very many examples of therapist limits manifesting, directly or indirectly, as requests for time out. The examples range from the therapist saying 'Excuse me, I need to close the window; the noise from the lawn mower distracts me' to apologising to the client for not having respected their own limits. It ranges from 'Sorry, I was a little late, I'll add five minutes to our session if you wish' to the therapist taking the initiative to inform a client that he or she can see a social worker about the financial worries that are preoccupying them, because the therapist finds it impossible to concentrate on the client's frame of reference before giving this information. If the therapist is focused on the limits on their ability to concentrate on the client's frame of reference, (classical client-centred) therapy is not taking place. It would be more correct to say that the therapist is doing whatever he or she finds necessary to get into a position where therapy – i.e. being fully present in experiencing unconditionally accepting empathic understanding of the client – can (again) take place.

Of course, clients also sometimes need to request time out from therapy: 'Before I forget, can you tell me where the social worker's office is?' or 'My mouth is so dry, could I have a glass of water, please?' These kinds of client question or request for time out are rarely problematic for the therapist and do not challenge any therapist limits. They are basically limits on the client's concentration on the job. But can one speak of 'the client's job'? An exploration of other kinds of client questions or requests for time out of therapy may be pertinent here.

Limits to answering client questions

Very broadly, one might say that the 'job' of the fully voluntary client in ordinary person-centred therapy is to concentrate, verbally or non-verbally, often through trial and error, on the concerns on which it necessary for them to concentrate in order to get closer to living 'the good life' – i.e. to live what for the client, not for anybody else, constitutes the good life. Put another way, most voluntary clients spend most of the time in therapy self-exploring and critically examining their way of living, often in particular their feelings and conduct in relationship with significant others, in order to find a more rewarding and satisfying way of living and to become the best they can be. It is this self-exploration that the therapist accompanies with unconditionally accepting empathic understanding, thereby ordinarily stimulating the client's further self-exploration and in-creased self-acceptance (Frankel, Rachlin & Yip-Bannicq, 2012).

Not infrequently, however, clients request time out from their self-exploration by turning to the therapist as an authority on this 'good life'. This is not surprising in light of Rogers' (1959: 213) second condition: 'That the first person, whom we shall term the client, is in a state of *incongruence*, being *vulnerable*, or *anxious*.' This implies that clients tend to have a relatively externalised focus of evaluation, and very many clients do indeed regard psychotherapists as experts on how to live the good life, as if a diploma in psychotherapy was synonymous with this expertise rather than a diploma in expertise on a certain way of relating with clients. Indeed, some therapists share this misconception of the kind of expertise they possess. For these therapists, it rarely poses a problem when clients turn to them for answers about how to live the good life, because they believe they have the answer and they believe they know how to guide the client to the good life. But for most therapists, particularly person-centred therapists, it poses a problem because they do not wish to be experts-on-the-client and because they are aware of the authority with which they are imbued by the medicalised culture of psychological services.

In the community of person-centred therapists, the issue of whether to answer client questions on what to do to get closer to the good life is controversial, even if very little has been written about it.

My awareness of the controversy comes mostly from my participation on the PCINTL e-mail network (see p. 7). In the discussions on this network it has become clear that most classically client-centred therapists join Barbara Brodley in recommending that the therapist does his or her best to answer client questions of whatever kind, accompanied by expressions of empathic understanding. Barbara Brodley (1995/2011: 240) wrote:

> Answering questions and being responsive to clients' requests in client-centred therapy are significant elements in our communication to clients of the therapist's respect and trust, communication of a deeply held nondirective attitude, and communication of the therapeutic attitudes. At our best, the interactions about clients' questions and requests come from as deep a source in ourselves as pure empathic interactions.

When discussing this on the e-mail network, Barbara Brodley often noted that not answering questions is similar to behaving like royalty with their subjects. Not answering questions implies a disrespectful put-down, a withholding of knowledge and therefore power, and consequent disempowerment of the client. This is completely counter to the equalisation of power between therapist and client that the therapist tries to create and maintain in person-centred therapy.

Rogers' own practice seems more varied. Sometimes he answered questions, sometimes he didn't. In April 2004 Barbara Brodley sent a message to the e-mail network with the following information:

> I am going to give you some findings from Claudia Kemps' PhD dissertation research. She is studying Rogers' responses to his clients' questions found from examining 129 interviews.

> These are findings only from the post-Bryan [Rogers, 1942] interviews (from 121 interviews, 1942 or 1943 through 1986). There are about 20 other sessions that were not available when Claudia began the analyses – thus not in the sample as well as the eight Mr Bryan sessions.

> *Findings:*

> Rogers responded with *answers* (not counting his acknowledgements without answer, and not counting

EURs [empathic understanding responses/empathic reflections]) to 51% of all 382 questions asked of him. We categorized 11 types of Q [questions].

Looking only at the 198 questions that ask Rogers for guidance, evaluation, opinion, perspective or permission (combining five of the categories):

- Rogers responded with answers to 37% of these questions.
- Rogers responded with empathic understanding responses (EURs) to 57% of these questions.
- Rogers responded with a combination of EURs and answers to 12% of these questions.

Rogers had very little to say on the subject of answering questions. In a comment to his demonstration interview with Peter Ann (Rogers, 1985) he said:

It is not stubbornness on my part that refuses to give any response, but it is a deep conviction that the best answer may come from within the client.

We can learn more about Rogers' practice with respect to answering questions from his transcribed interviews (Lietaer & Brodley, 2003):

Mrs Ett, 144: ... I can't imagine, though, why I should have this fear of windows, even after I would analyze it. Do you think perhaps that it will go away as I keep analyzing it in that same way, I mean, the fear? Does the change come overnight, or does it, is everything gradual –

Rogers, 144: We find people are very individual in that respect, but I do think there is a real chance of exploring it sufficiently to either find out what is the basis of it, or to help it assume a more normal proportion.

Mrs Ett, 145: Ah – what about sex behind all of these? Do you feel that there are some problems of sex that have to be, of a sexual nature shall we say that have to be, ah – probed, do you find that many times the feeling that I mentioned, this feeling of fear and guilt is in connection with a sexual, of a sexual nature, that is?

Rogers, 145: There again, I think that we would find people very individual, but I suppose that you are wondering somewhat about that yourself or you wouldn't have raised the question.

Mrs Ett, 146: Perhaps, yes. Either that or maybe I've read too many books (laugh). Can that enter into the picture too?

Rogers, 146: You're not quite sure whether you're – whether it's just an intellectualized notion, or if it's that there might be something of that in it, or whether it is your own feeling.

Mrs Ett, 147: Mhm. You keep tossing it back to me, don't you?

And that seems to me to be precisely what Rogers is doing – tossing Mrs Ett's questions back to her, and at the same time pretending to give the answers of an authority or expert on the subject: 'We find people are very individual.' There is, I think, much of the superior 'royal put-down' – or, in this case, even an imperial 'we' – that Barbara Brodley noted in this way of responding to client questions. It would have been so much better, I think, if Rogers had simply acknowledged that he didn't know the answer to Mrs Ett's questions.

In the following example Rogers does precisely that and the client easily accepts this and continues her self-exploration without further ado:

Mrs Roc, 27: Do you think this hook could have come up because I saw him?

Rogers, 27: I don't know. But I guess that's a question you're really wondering. 'Could it be because I went back to him or felt that relationship again?'

Mrs Roc, 28: Up to the time I saw him I was less clear. I was much more confused...

My own position with respect to answering client questions or responding to client requests for ideas, suggestions, advice etc is similar to Rogers' in this example: 'I'm sorry, I don't think I know. I do wish I did, because I can sure understand how helpful it would be for you, if I did,' or something to that effect. With increasing experience, my conviction that I have nothing helpful to offer from my own frame of reference has become ever more deeply held. When I first began to practise I did tend – tentatively of course – to answer client questions and accommodate their requests to be an expert on this or that issue that concerned them, but what I offered seldom seemed to be helpful. As time went on I became all the more convinced that I had nothing to offer beyond unconditionally accepting empathic understanding – apart from this, I simply didn't have any 'specialist' knowledge. I also learned that, in common with person-centred theory, in the end the answers and solutions clients came up with for themselves were a lot more creative, idiosyncratic and effective than anything I could have imagined. I deeply share Rogers' conviction (quoted above) 'that the best answer may come from within the client'. I'd actually go so far as to say that the best answer *does* come from within the client. For me, the issue is not that the therapist *should not* be an expert on the client; it is that the therapist *cannot* be an expert on the client (Sommerbeck, 2004).

However, some questions are about factual information that the client obviously needs, which I do have the answer to. Surely no therapist would decline to answer the question 'Where's the ladies room?' or 'How do I get to the social worker's office?' It would, of course, be decidedly unempathic, if not downright rude, not to answer these questions straightaway.

Clients, however, may have concerns in many areas, and therapists may feel that they do have some expertise in areas other than person-centred therapy, without in any way coming close to being an expert on the client. For my own part, I have knowledge of the workings of the psychiatric system in which I practised, the theory of client-centred therapy, doing psychological assessments, cooking, dog training and mathematics. When clients asked about the first (and they quite frequently did, because they were clients in that same psychiatric system), I very often thought I had an answer to their question, and in that case I felt it would have been close to criminal *not* to answer it. Indeed it often happened that I offered this kind of information without the client even having asked for it because I felt so sure it would be helpful and therapeutically relevant to them to know of it, and sitting on the information distracted me from empathising with the client. Clients have never asked me anything related to my other areas of expertise, so I have never offered information about them.

But, since I regard myself as somewhat of an expert on cooking, imagine, now, a client who mentions her regret that she is unable to make her husband's favourite dessert, lemon mousse, without sediment, which her husband detests. Do I know how to do it? Yes, I do happen to know how to avoid sediment in lemon mousse,[1] but I might not tell my client this because I don't know if that piece of

---

1. For interested readers, put the mousse in the freezer for 10 minutes before cooling it further in the fridge!

information would be useful to her. She has come to therapy because of marital problems; this piece of advice about the lemon mousse might help her to please her husband better as a housewife, but she might be better off giving up trying to please her husband in that way. I have no way of knowing, but telling her how to make lemon mousse without sediment seems to me to be endorsing a particular direction in her therapy and life towards becoming a more pleasing housewife/cook to her husband. In addition she might think that if she isn't interested in and doesn't follow my advice (the assumed authority on the good life), she might well incur my negative regard (Bower & Sommerbeck, 2013: 16).

She also asks questions about me and my life that I of course know the answer to, but I am puzzled as to why the client is asking them right now in this session. Do my husband and I have common interests or hobbies? The plain and factual answer to that is easy enough: yes, by and large. But again I might, from my perspective as a therapist, be more interested in why she needs to know this, or its therapeutic relevance to her, and request time out from therapy to ask about that, rather than answering the question. One reason for my hesitancy is, as already mentioned, that I do not know if the question is actually about how to live the good life, which I know absolutely nothing about.

It turns out that the client's husband's main interest happens to be one of my own – namely, mathematics – and he has tried to make her understand one of the basics of mathematics, Pythagoras' theorem, but she just doesn't get it, however hard she tries. At this point I do not say that I understand Pythagoras' theorem very well and could probably help her understand it. I certainly do not want to be perceived as conveying negative regard for her *not* understanding Pythagoras' theorem and I do not want to get into a teacher–pupil relationship with her. It was a good job that I didn't, because she later revealed that she was not at all interested in mathematics. She much preferred spending her spare time reading novels, and started to clarify to herself and consider telling her husband that she'd feel perfectly fine about not sharing their main interests, even if she believed as a general rule that most successful partnerships are based on common interests.

As this theme unfolded I accompanied much of it with empathic understanding, and all of it was material for her continued self-exploration so we got fluently back into therapy and I was pleased that I hadn't answered her question about my and my husband's interests. Actually, her question quickly evaporated into thin air, and she stopped feeling the need to know anything about my shared interests with my husband, or to understand Pythagoras' formula.

Both of these examples illustrate what the alarm bells in my head are trying to tell me when I am asked to disclose information about myself. The alarm bells warn me that I am, in effect, very probably being asked to convey conditional regard or to enter an extra-therapeutic relationship (see below) with the client. I may respond by empathically reflecting the client's question or I may try to find out what the question is about. Readers may remember that I did the first in my session with Marion:

M: Will you tell CP that I won't bring Douglas in, explain it to him?

T: For some reason you'd rather have me do it than do it yourself?

M: Yes, I'm afraid he'll be annoyed with me, because I won't bring Douglas in, but I'm sure he'd respect it if you told him.

T: Takes courage to say no to CP?

M: It sure does – I'm afraid he'll dismiss me from hospital soon, if I don't accept his proposal, so will you tell him?

T: You think that if I tell him, he won't dismiss you so soon?

M: Yes... Oh, why should that make a difference... It's just that sometimes it is a little difficult to talk with CP. He always seems to be in a hurry, a little impatient, and that makes me nervous. So I'd appreciate it, if you would talk with him?

T: You tend to feel nervous with CP, because you feel pressured when he seems to be in a hurry, and you'd prefer to avoid that by having me talk with him?

M: Yes, but... Well, I ought to do it myself. I'll talk with him myself.

T: You feel an obligation to do it yourself?

M: (Laughing) Yes, and I'm also a little annoyed with you, because I think you won't do it, but then I also just thought that this is the kind of situation I always try to avoid, saying no to others, and particularly to authorities, and it doesn't do me any good in the long run.

In this case, I could also have responded to Marion's question by refusing to do as she asked and giving my reasons for not wishing to accommodate her request – i.e. that it would have been confusing to have a relationship with her as her messenger/advocate in addition to my relationship with her as her therapist. (For more details about this example see comment 4, p. 59.)

The following example illustrates a question I have often come across but only rarely answered: 'Do you have children?' Here I know the answer too, of course, but rather than giving it I'd be interested in knowing about the client's need to know it or its therapeutic relevance. Is the client uncertain about having children although her partner wants children very much, and is she looking to me for some kind of guidance? Is she testing my acceptance (or not) of her preference to pursue her career rather than have children? Does she feel that she can only share with another mother problems she is having with her children that only another mother might accept and understand, and so on?

I have many memories of having become entangled in what some call the saviour/persecutor/victim triangle when I failed to consider sufficiently the potential consequences of answering clients' questions. I have, therefore, as far as I remember, only answered this apparently extremely simple question about my having children or not if the answer might have helped clients know how much they needed to tell me about the context to the problems they were describing in order for me to understand them. For example, knowing that I had a child of eight years would make it unnecessary for the client whose child was having problems at school to go into details about the education system. It's like someone asking you if you have read a particular book before discussing it; they may need first to explain what the book is about in order to be understood. In these cases, the client is in effect asking 'How much do you need to know in order to understand?' and I'd be perfectly willing to answer that question in order not to burden my client – and me – with any unnecessary exchange of information.

So I think there are good reasons for a therapist to request time out from therapy in order to try to find out what the consequences might be for the client of answering a question or not. And, as mentioned previously, the client asking a question can also be regarded as the client taking time out from therapy, so in this sense the therapist is accompanying the client in a shared time-out to discuss the question and the answering of it.

I am probably at variance with most person-centred therapists with respect to my being so cautious about answering questions. But my experience has confirmed Rogers' second condition (1959: 213), as I've discussed previously – that clients' locus of evaluation is externalised; they have learned by their experiences to become masters at sniffing out conditional regard in significant others, mostly people they regard as authorities, including the therapist. My fear is that answers, suggestions, advice etc that come from my own frame of reference will be received as authoritative, not in the light of their actual usefulness to the client. (Readers interested in a more detailed discussion of therapist self-disclosures in person-centred therapy are referred to Frankel & Sommerbeck, 2007b.)

On the other hand Barbara Brodley, in the first session, used to invite clients to ask her all the questions they wanted and would ordinarily answer them to the best of her ability, whatever they were about. Answers were often accompanied by empathic understanding responses (empathic reflection) (personal communication, 2002, and demonstration interview at the WAPCEPC conference in Egmond aan Zee, Netherlands, 6–11 July, 2003). Her extensive and carefully considered rationale (Brodley, 1997: 23–24; 2011, 55–57[2]) for this practice deserves a lengthy quote:

> Students sometimes assume that it is outside the scope of client-centered work to answer clients' questions or to honor clients' requests. Although incorrect, this conclusion is understandable because such behavior does risk influencing clients' choices, risks deflecting clients from their own exploratory process and risks undermining their self-direction. To avoid these risks of directive effects when their clients ask questions or make requests, some students of the approach tend to limit themselves to responding empathically to clients' feelings or motivations.
>
> Empathic responses, sometimes, may be an adequate response to a client's questions or requests. When a client asks a question or makes a request the therapist may feel the need to be sure he or she understands the client's subjective experience that has stimulated

---

2. I am grateful to Kathryn Moon for her permission to bring this quote from the collection of papers by Barbara T. Brodley that she published as first editor in 2011: Moon, K, Witty, M, Grant, B & Rice, B (eds)(2001).

the question or request. Or, the therapist may want to be sure the client meant the question as a question. In either case, an empathic response may be an adequate response from the client's point of view.

From the context of a question, the therapist often has enough information about the client's immediate frame of reference to have a basis for an accurate empathic understanding response, or at least for an empathic guess. Indeed, a client may feel a therapist's empathic response is more helpful than whatever answer the therapist might provide. If, however, the therapist's response to a client's intended question or request is limited to an empathic response, the client's intention – to be answered – has been ignored. The experience of being ignored, particularly if it occurs frequently, tends to diminish any person's sense of self and their sense of personal power in the situation.

There is a therapeutic problem even when clients do not object to their questions being left unanswered. Clients may interpret an empathic response as an avoidance of the question and, further, as indication that the therapist should not be asked questions. When this is the client's interpretation, the client's freedom of expression in the relationship has been diminished. An instance of avoidance of a client's question or request may not inhibit or disturb the client. If questions and requests are deflected by empathic responses frequently or systematically, however, the effect is likely to be one of disempowering the client to some extent. Any disempowerment of the client in client-centered therapy is viewed as counter-therapeutic.

Systematic avoidance of clients' questions and their requests is, effectively, a form of control over the therapeutic process and over the client. It diminishes the client's freedom to bring out his or her felt needs in the relationship. Diminished freedom may be the consequence of not responding directly to questions or requests even if the therapist is highly empathic to the client's motives and feelings and feels committed to empowerment.

> The nondirective attitude in client-centered work implies
> that questions and requests should be respected as
> part of the client's rights in the relationship. These rights
> are the client's right to self-determination of his or her
> therapeutic content and process, and the client's right
> to direct the manner of the therapist's participation
> within the limits of the therapist's philosophy, ethics
> and capabilities. The result of the therapist's respect
> towards these client rights is a collaborative therapeutic
> relationship (see Natiello, 1994).

It seems that my position and that of Barbara Brodley essentially differ with respect to the risks we accept and do not accept. Barbara Brodley would rather not risk being perceived as conveying directivity and power over the client; I'd rather not risk being perceived as conveying conditional regard for the client. Barbara Brodley would prefer to risk being perceived as conveying conditional regard in her answer to a question; I would rather risk being perceived as directing the client to not ask questions and so conveying conditional regard about asking questions, if it means I am not perceived as conveying conditional regard on anything else. And, as a matter of fact, I have indeed had clients who, sometimes smilingly and acceptingly, sometimes a little annoyed and resentful (Marion above, for example), have told me that they have given up asking me questions because they learned I wouldn't answer them. In the end most of them said they had come to appreciate it very much, because they found that, even if frustrating, it had helped them find their own answers and come to trust them. An exception is of course the client who asked me how I preferred to have sex with my husband and left, banging the door, when I refused to answer (p. 82).

You might ask if it is truly person-centred to consider the consequences for the client of answering questions (or accommodating requests). Do considerations like these not imply a step into the expert-on-the-client role? I think not. First, the therapist does not predict a consequence, as an expert-on-the-client therapist often does; the therapist just considers some imagined consequences in the light of Rogers' (1959: 213) second condition. Second, such considerations also take very seriously Rogers' sixth condition (ibid: 213), about the client perceiving the therapist's unconditional positive regard and empathic understanding, because these considerations represent the therapist's wish to reduce as far as possible the risk of being perceived as conveying conditional regard. In short, considering these issues means a consideration of all of Rogers' six necessary and sufficient conditions for therapeutic personality change that he listed in his 1959 chapter. This includes the client contributions to these conditions – they are not only considerations of the therapist's contributions of congruence, unconditional positive regard and empathic understanding.

In spite of Rogers' second condition, which implies the externalised locus of evaluation of the client, many – perhaps most – person-centred therapists rely on their clients to receive or reject what they offer from their own frame of reference in light of its actual usefulness to them, rather than regarding the therapist as an authority.

Doug Bower (Bower & Sommerbeck, 2013: 15) wrote:

> ... an important element on offering advice ... is based on the client's ability to decide to accept, reject, fail, or utilize any given assertion from a therapist. Withholding advice denies the client the opportunity to say 'no' or 'yes'.

And Art Bohart wrote (1995: 117):

> Later in the session, Andrea [who is wondering whether to re-establish a relationship with her former boyfriend, Lance] asked me whether I thought she should get reinvolved with Lance. I certainly did not know and disclosed my empathic sense of her confusion. 'If I were in your shoes I think I'd feel as confused as you. The scary part for me would be the fear I might make a wrong choice. I sense that may be true for you but I'm not sure. And you don't even know what's holding you back or whether or not it can be trusted.'

Marvin Frankel and I (2008: 73) expressed our concerns with respect to Art Bohart's response as follows:

> It is certainly directive in that it informs the client of the rightness of her fear because it is shared by her high-status therapist! It may be argued that in saying, 'If I were in your shoes I think I'd feel as confused as you ...' Bohart is being empathic since he is not directing the client on how to feel or what to do, but such an argument fails to recognize that Bohart is legitimatizing Andrea's confusion and not simply appreciating that that is how *she* feels.

Imagine a therapist legitimatizing a paranoid person's view of his boss by saying he or she would feel the same way in his shoes. The question whether the therapist would feel like the client, or not, were they actually in the client's shoes, has nothing to do with empathy and is therapeutically irrelevant ... However, Rogers ... with Gloria [Shostrom, 1965] does much the same as Bohart upon hearing how upset she is about her fear of taking risks. Rogers ... replies that 'life is risky' thus legitimatizing her anxieties as perfectly normal. This is a very risky thing to do (no pun intended) since for all we know, Andrea's description of her relationship with Lance may be highly distorted.

Art Bohart (2008: 85) wrote the following rejoinder:

As far as Frankel and Sommerbeck's contention that the response is authoritative, that is *their* perception, and they don't have the right to authoritatively decide for Andrea what her experience was. Frankel and Sommerbeck might argue that the power differential in therapy means clients like Andrea will not feel safe saying no, but they don't know my clients. Furthermore, they don't know the evolving context of therapy with Andrea, either. Clients are smart enough to pick up intentions over time. They can pick up how much a therapist really is nondirective in attitude, even if the therapist is not relying solely on empathic following responses...

Along the lines of Art Bohart's rejoinder, it is probably true for many therapists that limits on answering client questions and accommodating client requests are relaxed in the later phases of therapy. Still, how does the therapist know that the client is, indeed, in the later phases of therapy? It may seem so, and then turn out not to be so.

To conclude: in this section I hope I have succeeded in describing how varied the practice of person-centred therapists is with respect to answering questions and how controversial the issue is. No wonder that therapists often feel there are dilemmas involved – it would be worrying if they didn't!

Limits to therapist self-expression

In the section above, some of the examples were questions to the therapist about him- or herself: i.e. they were requests for therapist self-disclosure. I have given my reasons for very rarely answering such questions and the reasons of others for answering them. My reasons for not initiating self-disclosure – that is, talking about myself without being requested to do so by the client – would be the same: to minimise the risk of being perceived as conveying conditional regard. Here, again, I am at variance with many person-centred therapists. My practice is inspired by Rogers' early work, particularly by *Client-Centered Therapy* from 1951, whereas the practice of others is inspired by Rogers' later work, where therapist congruence is often taken to mean self-disclosure. From the discussion of the concept of congruence on p. 4, readers may remember the following quote by Rogers:

> When I am real in this fashion (genuine) I know that my own feelings will bubble up into awareness but be expressed in ways that won't impose themselves on my client. (Rogers, in Shostrom, 1965)

Many similar statements can be found in Rogers' later work and they have been influential for several prominent person-centred therapists. We have already mentioned Dave Mearns (p. 4), but with respect to the issue of self-disclosure or therapist self-expressiveness, Gill Wyatt (2001: 79–96) has been more explicit:

> A therapist's willingness to talk about their own experiences will mean the therapist is open to the experience of being vulnerable. If a therapist can successfully balance vulnerability, openness to learning, having their issues touched, *and* maintain professional and ethical practice, there are several advantages. A therapist's openness and acceptance of personal vulnerability may facilitate the client's acceptance of their vulnerability. The resultant mutuality between the therapist and client and the empowerment of the client appear surprising. By allowing himself to be vulnerable, and by allowing the client to teach him about his incongruence, our humanness, our sameness, the connection between two ordinary people is highlighted. (Ibid: 86)

Gill Wyatt gives the following example:

> I had often felt frustrated with John when I could not
> make contact with him. In the past I had chosen to tell
> him about my feelings as I thought I was picking up his
> unsymbolised experiences of feeling angry and although
> I expressed them as my own I hoped that he would
> recognise them and own his anger. I had stepped into
> the role of being the expert. Recently I realised that some
> or all of my anger is to do with my need for connection.
> When John withdraws – I miss that connection – it hurts
> and often I am unable to accurately symbolise my hurt
> or fear and only symbolise and communicate my anger.
> Having understood this, the next time John withdrew
> and I felt my frustration – I looked at *the edges of my*
> *awareness* and found my fear, my disappointment, my
> yearning for deep connection. The intensity of this was
> due to my unresolved incongruences, not to do with John,
> yet I felt it was important to say to John that when I looked
> a little closer at my frustration I also found I missed him
> and felt a little scared. John looked at me and said, 'I miss
> myself.' (Ibid: 86, original emphasis)

I'll certainly not deny that clients can be helped by therapist self-expression, as seems to have been the case with John. Nevertheless, in my opinion Gill Wyatt ran a disproportionate risk of being perceived as conveying conditional regard by telling this withdrawn client that she missed him – that is, conditional regard of his withdrawnness. I have, however, other reasons for being sceptical about Gill Wyatt's position: I am very doubtful about the therapeutic importance of 'the connection between two ordinary people'. The client has searched out the therapist in his or her role precisely as a therapist and may very likely already have spoken in vain with several 'ordinary people'. And yearning for deep connection may not correspond with the client's yearnings. The very fragile clients of psychiatry are mostly decidedly scared of 'deep connection' and it is important that the therapist feels comfortable with and accepting of a 'shallow connection'. This critique could of course also be levelled at the idea of working at relational depth (Mearns & Cooper, 2005).

I imagine Gill Wyatt (and Dave Mearns) would have responded to my critique along the lines of Carl Whitaker's comments on Rogers' way of practising with his clients in the Wisconsin Project:

If one assumes the process of therapy is in the person of the *therapist* then the life theme of the therapist should be an essential characteristic and visible in any segment of verbal recording. I would formulate our theme as: the therapist says by his total functioning, 'I am trying to grow, come we'll both work at it together.' I cannot see the personal theme of these therapists. I expect to enjoy the patient. I expect to respond only if I feel emotionally spontaneous or if there is some necessity for restructuring the relationship. The Rogerians here seem committed to respond at each point of the patient's verbalization. I watch and wait for the encounter. They seem to make an effort to start an encounter with each move of the patient. I feel that therapy is an opportunity and a responsibility for joining with the patient in an interaction around my convictions, possibly not in moral issues but in the issues of interpretation and evaluation of the current experience and possibly even of his historical experience. I feel free to challenge the patient if I feel personally related to what is going on. I do not feel this is true of the therapists here portrayed... The lack of spontaneity and the lack of flexibility in the therapist-as-a-person seemed an orientation very much like analysis. The therapist is standing behind the patient, unseen and almost non-existent. Does this denial of self actually imply an acknowledgment of the 'other'? Is it possible that the patient is being taught to be more on guard because the therapist is so on guard? What is the effect of the therapist not enjoying his relationship with his patient; of not being able to express himself personally? (Rogers et al, 1967: 510–11, original emphasis)

Gill Wyatt, however, is also cautious with respect to therapist self-expression:

One concern regarding incongruent self-expression [and it may be remembered from p. 5 that the therapist cannot know whether his or her self-expression is congruent or not] or inappropriate therapist behaviour is that the therapist subtly controls the therapeutic process in order to satisfy their own needs, reflecting misuse, and, in extreme cases, abuse of therapeutic power. Another concern is that by the therapist keeping access to their

own frame of reference and sometimes expressing
themselves from their frame of reference they will
become an expert and the client's ability to self-direct will
become thwarted. It is the responsibility of each therapist
to self-reflect and self-monitor these concerns. (Wyatt,
2001: 91)

Again, the issue of limits with respect to therapist expression is
complex and controversial. Rogers' statement with respect to suicide
might also fit here:

These are deep issues, which strike to the very core of
therapy. They are not issues which one person can decide
for another. Different therapeutic orientations have acted
upon different hypotheses. All that one person can do is
to describe his own experience and the evidence which
grows out of that experience. (Rogers, 1951: 48)

Limits to extra-therapeutic relationships with clients

Most therapists prefer not to have extra-therapeutic relationships of
any kind with their clients, regardless of particular professional limits,
which might vary slightly over time. In most cases (for exceptions, see
below), therapists experience a clear boundary between therapeutic
and extra-therapeutic relationships and will normally decline invi-
tations from clients to enter into an extra-therapeutic relationship
with them and also not initiate extra-therapeutic relationships with
clients themselves.

There seem to be good reasons for this preference. Barbara
Brodley (1975/2011: 45) wrote:

Clients (and therapists) are *at their best* – they are more
fair-minded, more reflective, more understanding, tolerant
and accepting, more accommodating and intelligent – in
therapy than anywhere else. *The client's presentation of
his worst characteristics is responsible, humane, critical,
undefensive, and reflective in the therapy situation.
Demands upon the client by the therapist are very
circumscribed.* The therapist can deceive himself into
thinking this very attractive client can 'hold up' in other
situations, at least with him. And can deceive himself
into thinking he can be as accepting and understanding
in his natural habitat as he is in the more limited therapy

situation. It's very unlikely that the therapist can do so because getting out of [the therapy situation] *leads to a loss of the functional equality of client and therapist built up by the therapist. The inequality reasserts itself. The client loses a good therapist and is likely to get hurt when he finds he cannot hold up his end of a relationship* (even if the therapist friend is not holding up his end either).

Following up on Barbara Brodley's concerns, we can look at an imagined example.

A client is taking the, for him, very daring step of, for the first time, playing the trumpet in a small jazz band at a public concert. He hopes to become a professional trumpet player so this is a very important event for him. He tells the therapist how nervous he is, and that it would feel very calming and supportive for him if the therapist would come to the concert and the reception afterwards, which he also feels nervous about. He would of course pay all expenses: this is also an invitation. The therapist happens to like jazz very much, and also hopes the client, for whom she cares deeply, will succeed in his career ambitions. So she sees no good reasons to reject the invitation and accepts it. And it may indeed turn out very well – the client may be a success, the event may be a turning point in his life, and he may partly give credit for this to the therapist's supporting him by coming to the concert. The therapist may not be 100% satisfied with this credit, but that is such a minor issue compared with the decisive turn for the better of the client's whole life. A true 'miracle moment' (in the so-called recovery movement of psychiatry survivors the importance of a helper doing something out of the ordinary, something extra that is not included in his or her professional role, is often mentioned as a decisive turning point in their voyage towards recovery).

But things could have turned out in a very different way. The therapist might not have liked the client's way of playing the trumpet, might have found it to be rather staccato and poor standard; or afterwards, at the reception, the therapist might have disliked the client interrupting others all the time and swallowing handfuls of snacks in between a seemingly endless number of drinks. In short, the therapist might end up feeling judgmental and distancing of the client and, with these feelings, the event was not at all enjoyable for her. And, following this, she lied to the client: she praised his playing when he asked about it, as one can prefer to do at purely social events with rather distant acquaintances. She feared the next session with him: 'How shall I feel unconditional acceptance of him again?', 'Did he perceive my judging him so he will no longer believe in my unconditional acceptance of him, even if/when I rescue this experience?', and 'What may be his next expectation of me with regard to extra-therapeutic relationships?' All this is another way for a therapist to become entangled in the saviour/persecutor/ victim triangle that was described on p. 25. Is the risk of becoming entangled in this triangle worth the possibility of a 'miracle moment'? In my experience, miracle moments are rare. Therapeutic personality change much more often comes about through a slow, almost inconspicuous process.

What then about inserting a therapeutic relationship into an already existing extra-therapeutic relationship? Here is what Barbara Brodley (1975/2011: 45) had to say on this issue:

> It is much easier and more workable to take a person
> you already know, love, have sex with, and work with,
> into therapy than to go in the other direction. You both
> already know about the limitations of each other in
> the personal relationship and can find the therapist
> exchange an improvement for both people, as well as
> having effects that reverberate back into the original,
> ongoing relationship.

This matches my own experience completely. I have often offered a brief course of therapy to psychiatric nurses, who were also my colleagues, when they were traumatised by, for example, having been exposed to violence by a patient or by one of their patients having taken their own life. It has also happened a few times that my manager asked me to be the therapist of a colleague whose private problems were threatening her capacity to continue working, and I never refused such a request. I have never had any problematic experiences doing this kind of work; on the contrary. During the years, it developed into one of my formal work roles that I should also be 'a carer of the carers' and this was much appreciated by my colleagues, as well as by me. For me it meant a welcome opportunity to work with well-functioning clients, an opportunity that strengthened my confidence in my practice with the ordinary clients of psychiatry, where progress was much slower and less noticeable.

In spite of the positive experiences I have had when doing therapy with colleagues, this practice would generally be frowned upon or even not allowed by the codes of ethics of most professional bodies. And there are good reasons for this. Maybe I have simply been lucky: things might not have turned out well if, say, the client/ colleague had been dissatisfied with the therapy with me, or if I had learned something during the therapy that strained the colleague relationship. So the wisdom of my practice is worth discussing and, in any case, referral to provider organisations like employee assistance programmes has become increasingly common. Nevertheless, if need be, I think I'd probably again do my best to help a friend/colleague rather than adhere to some external rule of conduct with respect to this issue.

Sometimes an extra-therapeutic relationship with a client occurs by accident and cannot be avoided. This mostly occurs in small communities where the therapist is likely to run into clients in the street, shops, restaurants and the like. I have worked in small communities, and these accidental meetings have rarely posed any problems. The client and I have exchanged greetings and perhaps a little small talk about the weather and then we have continued each on our own way. Occasionally a client has rushed over to me, in a restaurant for example, and started talking with me as if we were in session. In these cases, I have, as kindly as possible, referred the client to our next session, perhaps acknowledging their need to talk by offering an earlier session than originally scheduled, and then used part of the next session to check how the client felt about my rejection and to explain that I, for various reasons, couldn't offer therapy in that accidental setting: I felt too tired after a long day's work; I had to attend to the company I was with; I couldn't eat and practise therapy at the same time; I didn't like practising in public etc. I cannot remember any incident of this nature that I did not sort out satisfactorily in my next meeting with the client.

Occasionally I would see a client when out and about in the community and they did not greet me, even though I knew they had seen me. This raised another dilemma. Did the client want me to greet them? Or did they not want me to show that they knew me? Many clients do not tell anybody that they are having, or have in the past had, contact with the psychiatric system, and might be offended or embarrassed if I greeted them, particularly when in company with others. Mostly I would not take the initiative to greet a client I met accidentally, but would explain why in the next session and ask if they wanted to be greeted or not if we met like this again. I don't remember any client who did not appreciate my saying this, and tell me what they preferred. But still, when it happened, it felt uncomfortable to me and I would request time out from therapy to discuss with the client the consequences of these accidental extra-therapeutic meetings.

With very contact-impaired, withdrawn clients, there may, however, sometimes be good reasons for having what, at first glance at least, seems like an extra-therapeutic or even a comrade-like relationship. I hinted at this above when I spoke about some of these clients having difficulty tolerating the intimacy of an encounter that concentrates on them, rather than on 'a common third party, activity or event'. Typically, these are clients whom the therapist approaches on his or her own initiative while engaging in a shared activity with them, like noticing the surroundings on a walk in the park, piecing together a puzzle, making a cup of tea or whatever might have a chance of leading them to be engaged. Of course, this also implies answering questions, which will typically be concrete questions about the shared activity or common third party: not all questions to a supposed therapist-authority are about how to live the good life. As a matter of fact, contact-impaired clients often do not even regard such comradely shared activity as therapy, and even less do they regard the therapist as an authority. When they start to do that, their contact capacities have improved. Correspondingly, I regard this activity as person-centred *practice* rather than person-centred *therapy* (Sommerbeck, 2003: 20). Others have termed it 'contact work' (Sanders, 2007). With these contact-impaired clients the therapist will also typically use pre-therapy responses during their shared activity. In his writings about 'wilderness therapy' Rab Erskine (2015) has given very vivid accounts of how he combines shared, comradely activities with pre-therapy.

Another good reason for entering into an extra-therapeutic relationship with a client, or, rather, substituting the psychotherapeutic relationship with another kind of helping relationship, has to do with the politics of psychotherapy (Proctor et al, 2006). Psychotherapy tends to individualise problems by focusing on change in the individual and does not take much heed of all the environmental and political factors that are major contributors to psychological distress, such as poverty, bad housing, unemployment, discrimination etc. In a sense, it could be said that these factors are societal expressions of negative regard for the individual and just as important for the development of psychological problems as the negative regard of significant others with which psychotherapy, including person-centred therapy, mostly deals. And, although the person-centred approach has clear political implications (Bozarth, 1998; Proctor et al, 2006), Rogers did not take societal oppression into consideration in his theory of personality (Rogers, 1959: 221–34). So it is perhaps fair enough that Skinner's deterministic theory, rather than Rogers' theory of internally motivated self-actualisation, won the American Humanist Association 'Humanist of the Year' award in 1972 (Sommerbeck, 2011).

Of course, person-centred therapists hope that clients will be better able to deal with societal expressions of negative regard at the end of therapy – at the very least, that clients will no longer internalise them but see them for what they are. However, there are cases of clients being referred to therapy where it rather quickly becomes evident that therapy is not the best kind of helping relationship for the client. Getting a job with the help of a competent social worker might increase the self-worth of a client better and more quickly than therapy. A four-room apartment instead of just two rooms may relieve tension in a family of six better than a course of family therapy. The overweight teenager referred to therapy may be helped better by a compassionate schoolteacher who encourages his or her schoolmates to recognise their intelligence rather than bully them for being overweight, and so on.

In these cases, the issue of therapist limits becomes synonymous with the limits of therapy itself: the client might be better helped by the therapist discussing this with them, possibly leading to a referral to another kind of helping relationship. Alternatively, the therapist may have another kind of relevant helping expertise and engage in another kind of helping relationship with the client, instead of the psychotherapeutic relationship. Doing this might also be frowned upon and possibly be considered unethical; nevertheless I did it, not infrequently, and without qualms.

For example, as a clinical psychologist in a psychiatric hospital, one of my functions was also to do psychological assessments. It could then happen that a new (therapy) client, as well as the reports accompanying their referral, disclosed that they had been in therapy several times before, to no avail, and each time they had been referred by the social authorities in order to avoid approving the client's application for disability pension. In these cases, in Denmark at least, the client's own words are not trusted. Instead the social services require endless documentation from professionals – experts – in order to decide whether to accept the client's application. They also tend to require clients to go through all kinds of 'treatments' in the hope that they can avoid accepting the client's application. It is worth noting that this whole process often ends up costing a lot more than if they had accepted the client's application much earlier.

Whenever I learned that a new client was struggling with this problem, I would offer to do a psychological assessment instead of doing therapy, as I was almost certain, from the papers and my impression of the client, that this would help their application. Invariably the client responded with relief and we did the assessment, and mostly it was supportive of the client's application. The client's psychiatrist was also usually very relieved that they didn't have to keep changing the client's medication to see if this or that psychoactive drug worked better than the previous one (and, in my experience, a change in medication never made any positive difference). The expert psychiatrist then wrote a report that all therapeutic possibilities had been tried to no avail; that the expert psychological assessment, which was included; demonstrated more serious mental distress than had hitherto appeared, and that the client's application for disability pension should therefore be accepted.

Such reports were usually acted on, and we didn't see most of these clients in the psychiatric system again. With a stable income that lifted them out of poverty, they could apparently live the relatively peaceful life they had wanted for such a long time. A few of them did ask for proper psychotherapy because they discovered that they actually did want to be able to work again; they just couldn't concentrate on therapy when they were constantly stressed by having to live from hand to mouth. Some of these clients succeeded after a long course of therapy in coming off their disability pension and getting back to work; others decided that they were indeed disabled, no matter how much they tried to change this, and accepted their disability pension more wholeheartedly.

I imagine that other therapists could tell similar stories of lending their own 'expert voice' to clients in situations where social services do not trust the client's own voice. In this particular example of an extra-therapeutic relationship with a client, what mattered was that I did indeed possess an expert voice (expertise in psychological assessment) in the eyes of the social services and of course also in my own eyes. I was not allowing the client to lean on any illusory expertise in living the good life, as was the case with some of the examples of extra-therapeutic relationships mentioned earlier in this section. It is also noteworthy that this extra-therapeutic relationship was an alternative to therapy right at the start of my relationship with the client and that only a few clients wanted to start a therapeutic relationship with me when the extra-therapeutic relationship ended. With these few, the transition was not difficult. This probably confirms Barbara Brodley's assertion (p. 90) that it is mostly unproblematic to go from an extra-therapeutic relationship to a therapeutic relationship, whereas it can be very problematic to go in the other direction.

Limits and Referrals

Potentially all the limits described on the previous pages might result in a referral or a recommendation to the client to seek help elsewhere instead of, or in conjunction with, seeing the therapist. In addition, as we saw above, there are reasons for seeking help to which therapy is not, at least not directly, the answer – for example, the distress caused by being homeless, poor, unemployed, bullied, discriminated against, being the victim of violence etc. Likewise, there are symptoms that masquerade as those of psychological problems but are in reality symptoms of a physical illness or side effects of some medication. Although therapy may in some of these cases indirectly enable clients to benefit more from the help that other professionals can offer them more directly with respect to these problems. They may for example find better ways to live with an illness or they may become empowered to stand up better for their rights.

Nevertheless, any limit may end up with the therapist convinced that he or she can be of no use to the client, either in the first session or at a later point in the course of therapy. In this case hopefully the therapist will know of other people who they believe can help the client and refer or recommend them accordingly. Sanders and colleagues (2009: 262–63) speak of the importance of developing a 'referral network' of people with more and/or different areas of experience and expertise to those of the therapist, with other therapeutic orientations and with various extra-therapeutic competences that may be needed to help the client. Alternatively, if therapists are educated in two therapeutic orientations or have a required extra-therapeutic competence, they might in some circumstances refer to themselves, so to speak. For example, having been trained in cognitive behavioural therapy, I have been able to switch to this mode of therapy with clients who evidently wanted a more directive approach and I have been unable to help them with person-centred therapy. Likewise, I have sometimes, as already described, 'referred to myself' in my capacity of psychological assessor to support a client's application for disability benefit (see p. 32.)

Sometimes it is a straightforward process to make a referral or recommendation and sometimes it is not. The latter is mostly the case when the idea of referral or recommendation comes from the therapist and has not occurred to the client. In this case the referral or recommendation implies in essence that the therapist is stepping into the role of expert-on-the-client and making a critique or judgment on the client's expectation that the therapist can help him or her, and this is so whether the client welcomes the therapist taking this role or not. Thus, the therapist has to carefully consider the pros and cons of making a referral or recommendation and in all cases make it very tentatively. From the outset, of course, the therapist cannot know if the referral or recommendation will benefit the client or not.

In addition sometimes it is easy for the therapist to be honest about the reason for making a referral and sometimes it is not. If the reason for a referral or recommendation is a personal limit of the therapist's, it is likely to be more difficult to be honest about it, and it also has to be taken into consideration that honesty for honesty's own sake may do more harm than good.

Here is an example from my own practice that illustrates some of the difficulties that may be uncomfortably pertinent when making a referral or recommendation, because of a personal limit of the therapist. I had seen a client, an inpatient in the psychiatric hospital where I worked, for five or six sessions. At that point I began to become aware that I might not be able to help him. He was an Inuit from Greenland and, as the case is for most 'Southern Danes', it was almost impossible for me to read his body language and facial expressions. In fact, to me he actually seemed to have none. As a consequence I felt very distant from him and there was hardly any empathic understanding to speak of in my relationship with him. Nevertheless, he wished to continue coming to see me and actually said that he liked our talks, even if he didn't say much.

As this state of affairs continued, I took my problem to supervision and, as a result, decided to ask him if he felt helped by the therapy. If not, I would refer him to an Inuit private therapist and ask the hospital to pay for this. I had conflicting thoughts and feelings about this decision. Should I not continue when he wanted to come? Was it not an expression of lack of trust in him to suggest a referral? On the one hand, I felt it was. On the other, I felt utterly unable to help him and that it would amount to deceiving him if I went on. Furthermore, I had started to dread the sessions with him because I felt so incompetent with him, and this was certainly not conducive to good therapy; indeed, it meant very much the reverse.

I was also concerned that he would perceive this as a case of the discrimination against their Inuit countrymen that is not uncommon among Southern Danes. The decision was indeed a result of my not being able to deal with diversity, with our differing ethnicities, and I felt embarrassed and ashamed. So for these many reasons I was distressed about my decision to refer him elsewhere. But, no matter how much I turned it around in my head, it remained the right decision. Continuing the therapy would only have meant going from bad to worse, increasing the deception and in all likelihood doing damage to the client, to me and to the reputation of the hospital (see also Sanders, 2011: 115).

So, at our next session I asked him if he felt helped by the therapy and he answered no, but said he thought it would change in time. I told him I felt sure it would not and suggested the referral, and was honest about my reasons for it. At first he accepted it politely but I did manage to help him also express some of the grievance, anger and sadness that he actually felt at my coming to this decision and my reasons for it. He did feel somewhat rejected and discriminated against and I did not fully manage to communicate my decision in a way that left him, in Pete Sanders' phrase (ibid: 121), feeling a precious gift rather than an awkward bundle.

The non-expert stance in the relationship with the client is important to most person-centred therapists but cannot always be adopted when it comes to referrals for problems that originate in the limits of what therapy as such may accomplish, rather than in the personal limits and limits of competence of the therapist. In some cases the contribution of a social worker, occupational therapist, lawyer etc may be more helpful. Very often the therapist will be more of an expert than the client on the whole helping system and will know more about where to go for help that therapy can't offer, and how best to get it – help with money, housing, employment, legal matters and the like. In these instances adopting the expert-on-the-client stance is also supported by the fact that many professionals will only accept referrals from third-party professionals, who are assumed to be experts on the client and expected to advocate for the client. I think it goes without saying that the therapist should accept that they have this expertise and use it in collaboration with clients whenever relevant. To my mind it would be quite unethical to 'treat' the often very distressing consequences of poverty, unemployment etc exclusively with psychotherapy. To do so sends an implicit message to the client that their plight is the result of their own individual psychological problems or even illness – a message that says, in essence, 'It's your own fault.' Some political factions may hold this view but it is judgmental of the client and cannot be reconciled with unconditional positive regard for the client and therefore with person-centred therapy. The person-centred therapist must use their expertise to refer the client to whatever professional or agency they know can help them with these kinds of problems.

However, making these referrals may be easier said than done. It is not always straightforward and simple to determine when the referral is relevant or not. It may appear relevant to the therapist but be irrelevant to the client. If the therapist then suggests a referral, there is the risk – as is the case with almost all suggestions from the therapist's own perspective, however well intentioned – that the client may experience it as judgmental. For example, a client of mine had the problem, among others, that her ex-husband did not keep to their access arrangements for the children: when they were to stay with him, when he'd fetch them, when he'd bring them back etc. She described this state of affairs as being confusing and frustrating, not least for the children, and there was also a certain degree of disappointment and sadness involved for all of them.

She and her ex-husband had joint custody of the children and had agreed their arrangements with no legal involvement. She said that she now regretted this; that she would feel better with legally binding agreements or, perhaps even better, with having sole custody. Hearing about this, I naturally thought of the very excellent lawyer that the hospital usually recommended in cases like this. I could easily refer her to this lawyer and she could consult with him free of charge, because this was a question of the children's welfare. It seemed so obvious that I should suggest this referral, but some sixth sense made me hesitate – or perhaps it was not a sixth sense, because I did wonder why she had not already found legal help herself. She was well educated and informed, so I thought she knew she was entitled to free legal consultation in her circumstances. It turned out to be fortunate that I had hesitated, because she soon after disclosed that she had indeed thought of getting legal help but was very ambivalent about it because she didn't want to do anything that might put her ex-husband off; she still loved him and hoped that they might re-establish their marriage. So she was actually very conflicted in her relationship with her children and her ex-husband, and she spent much time in therapy exploring this conflict and whether not seeking sole custody would harm the children.

Thus, even if making a referral seems self-evident, it may not actually be so, and therapist sensitivity and concerns about client experience of acceptance and understanding are as appropriate with respect to this limit of therapy as they are to any other.

Closing Comments

Readers who have followed me all the way to these closing comments will have surely become aware that I belong to the classical client-centred tribe of the person-centred nation (Sanders, 2004) and that this book is written on the basis of my experiences of practising classical client-centred therapy in a psychiatric context. I have, however, done my best to also represent the views of person-centred therapists who do not identify as belonging to this tribe and whose working contexts and client groups are different from mine. I doubt I have done this to their full satisfaction, so I hope the book will stimulate them to write much more about limits from their own perspectives.

My intention has been to encourage readers to take seriously and respect their experiences of limits in their person-centred practice and inspire them to clarify their own position on limits and their own rationales for them. I hope I have managed to convey the complexity of the issue, and the many controversies inherent in it.

In closing, I return yet again to Rogers' statement with regard to limits in person-centred practice:

> These are deep issues, which strike to the very core of therapy. They are not issues which one person can decide for another. Different therapeutic orientations have acted upon different hypotheses. All that one person can do is to describe his own experience and the evidence which grows out of that experience. (Rogers, 1951: 48)

This book is my description of my experience and the evidence that grew out of that experience.

References

Adams C (2012) Presentation about therapist self-defence at WAPCEPC conference in Antwerp.

Axline V (1969) *Play Therapy*. New York: Ballantine.

Baldwin M (2000) Interview with Carl Rogers on the use of self in therapy. In: M Baldwin (ed) *The Use of Self in Therapy*. New York: Haworth (pp. 29–38).

Barrett-Lennard G (1998) *Carl Rogers' Helping System: Journey and substance*. London: Sage Publications.

Bohart A (1995) The person-centered psychotherapies. In: A Gurman, S Messer (eds) *Essential Psychotherapies*. New York: Guilford Press.

Bohart A (2008) Response to Frankel and Sommerbeck. *The Person-Centered Journal* 15(1–2): 83–8.

Bower D, Sommerbeck L (2013) From nondirective to nonpredictive. *The Person-Centered Journal* 20(1–2): 3–19.

Bozarth J (1990) The essence of client-centered therapy. In: G Lietaer, J Rombauts, R Van Balen (eds) *Client-centered and Experiential Psychotherapy in the Nineties*. Leuven: Leuven University Press.

Bozarth J (1998) *Person-centered Therapy: A revolutionary paradigm*. Ross-on-Wye: PCCS Books.

Brodley BT (1975/2011) Ethics in psychotherapy. In: K Moon, M Witty, B Grant, B Rice (eds) (2011) *Practicing Client-centered Therapy: Selected writings of Barbara Temaner Brodley*. Ross-on-Wye: PCCS Books (pp. 33–47).

Brodley BT (1997/2011) Considerations when responding to questions and requests in client-centred therapy. In: K Moon, M Witty, B Grant, B Rice (eds) (2011) *Practicing Client-centered Therapy: Selected writings of Barbara Temaner Brodley*. Ross-on-Wye: PCCS Books (pp. 55–7).

Brodley BT (1997) The nondirective attitude in client-centered therapy. *The Person-Centered Journal* 4(1): 18–30.

Brodley BT (1998) Criteria for making empathic responses in client-centered therapy. *The Person-Centered Journal* 5(1): 20–8.

Cooper D (1967) *Psychiatry and Anti-psychiatry*. London: Tavistock.

Dorfman E (1951) Play therapy. In: C Rogers (ed) *Client-centered Therapy*. Boston: Houghton Mifflin (pp .235–27).

Ellinwood C, Raskin N (1993) Client-centered/humanistic psychotherapy. In: T Kratochwill, R Morris (eds) *Handbook of Psychotherapy with Children and Adolescents*. Boston: Allyn & Bacon (pp. 264–375).

Erskine R (2015) To be published in *Person-Centred & Experiential Psychotherapies* no 3 or 4.

Frankel M, Sommerbeck L (2005) Two Rogers and congruence: the emergence of therapist-centered therapy and the demise of client-centered therapy. In: B Levitt (ed) *Embracing Non-directivity*. Ross-on-Wye: PCCS Books (pp. 40–62).

Frankel M, Sommerbeck L (2007a) Two Rogers: congruence and the change from client-centered therapy to we-centered therapy. *Person-Centered & Experiential Psychotherapies* 6(4): 286–95.

Frankel M, Sommerbeck L (2007b) Training and supervision of Rogers-1 and Rogers-2 counsellors. In: K Tudor, M Worrall (eds) *Freedom to Practise II: Person-centred approaches to supervision*. Ross-on-Wye: PCCS Books.

Frankel M, Sommerbeck L (2008) Nondirectivity: an attitude or a practice? *The Person-Centered Journal* 15(1–2): 58–78.

Frankel M, Rachlin H, Yip-Bannicq M (2012) How nondirective therapy directs: the power of empathy in the context of unconditional positive regard. *Person-Centered & Experiential Psychotherapies* 11(3): 205–15.

Gendlin E (1967) Therapeutic procedures in dealing with schizophrenics. In: C Rogers, E Gendlin, D Kiesler, C Truax (1967) *The Therapeutic Relationship with Schizophrenics*. Madison, WI: University of Wisconsin Press (pp. 369–401).

Harrison M (2011) How to get from CCT to RD and even CBT, without moving. *Person-Centred Quarterly* May.

Hart JT, Tomlinson TM (eds) (1970) *New Directions in Client-Centered Therapy*. Boston: Houghton Mifflin.

Lietaer G (1993) Authenticity, congruence and transparency. In: D Brazier (ed) *Beyond Carl Rogers*. London: Constable and Company (pp. 17–46).

Lietaer G, Brodley BT (2003) Carl Rogers in the therapy room: a listing of session transcripts and a survey of publications referring to Rogers' sessions. *Person-Centered & Experiential Psychotherapies* 2(4): 274–92.

Mearns D (1994) *Developing Person-Centred Counselling*. London: Sage Publications.

Mearns D, Cooper M (2005) *Working at Relational Depth in Counselling and Psychotherapy*. London: Sage Publications.

Moon K (2001) Nondirective client-centered therapy with children. *The Person-Centered Journal* 8(1): 43–53.

Moon K, Witty M, Grant B, & Rice, B (eds) (2011) *Practicing Client-centered Therapy: Selected writings of Barbara Temaner Brodley*. Ross-on-Wye: PCCS Books

Natiello P (1994) The collaborative relationship in psychotherapy. *The Person-Centered Journal* 1(2): 11–8.

Pearce P, Sommerbeck L (eds) (2014) *Person-Centred Practice at the Difficult Edge*. Monmouth: PCCS Books.

Proctor G, Cooper M, Sanders P, Malcolm B (eds) (2006) *Politicizing the Person-Centred Approach: An agenda for societal change.* Ross-on-Wye: PCCS Books.

Prouty G (1994) *Theoretical Evolutions in Person-Centered/Experiential Therapy: Applications to schizophrenic and retarded psychoses.* Westport CT: Praeger.

Prouty G, Van Werde D, Pörtner M (2002) *Pre-therapy: Reaching contact-impaired clients.* Ross-on-Wye: PCCS Books.

Rogers C (1942) *Counseling and Psychotherapy.* Boston: Houghton Mifflin.

Rogers, C (1951) *Client-Centered Therapy.* Boston: Houghton Mifflin.

Rogers C (1957) The necessary and sufficient conditions of therapeutic personality change. *Journal of Consulting Psychology* 21(2): 95–103.

Rogers C (1959) A theory of therapy, personality, and interpersonal relationships as developed in the client-centered framework. In: E Koch (ed) *Psychology: A study of a science.* Vol. 3. New York: McGraw-Hill.

Rogers C (1985) Demonstration interview with Peter Ann at the Evolution of Psychotherapy conference, Phoenix, Arizona. [Online.] http://www.youtube.com/watch?v=vAeXCn7_ji8

Rogers C (1987) Transference. *Person-Centered Review* 2(2): 182–8.

Rogers C, Gendlin E, Kiesler D, Truax C (1967) *The Therapeutic Relationship with Schizophrenics.* Madison, WI: University of Wisconsin Press.

Sachse R (2004) From client-centered to clarification-oriented psychotherapy. *Person-Centered & Experiential Psychotherapies* 3: 19–35.

Sanders P (ed) (2004) *The Tribes of the Person-Centred Nation.* Ross-on-Wye: PCCS Books.

Sanders P (ed) (2007) *The Contact Work Primer.* Ross-on-Wye: PCCS Books.

Sanders P (2011) *First Steps in Counselling* (4th ed). Ross-on-Wye: PCCS Books.

Sanders P, Frankland A, Wilkins P (2009) *Next Steps in Counselling Practice* (2nd ed). Ross-on-Wye: PCCS Books.

Sanders P, Hill A (2014) *Counselling for Depression: A person-centred and experiential approach to practice.* London: Sage.

Shlien J (1957) Time-limited psychotherapy: an experimental investigation of practical values and theoretical implications. *Journal of Consulting Psychology* 9(318): 15–22.

Shostrom E (ed) (1965) Client-centered therapy. In: *Three Approaches to Psychotherapy* [film]. Orange, CA: Psychological Films.

Sommerbeck L (2003) *The Client-Centred Therapist in Psychiatric Contexts: A therapist's guide to the psychiatric landscape and its inhabitants.* Ross-on-Wye: PCCS Books.

Sommerbeck L (2004) Non-linear dynamic systems and the non-directive attitude in client-centered therapy. *Person-Centered & Experiential Psychotherapies* 3(4): 291–9.

Sommerbeck L (2011) Bridging the positions of Rogers and Skinner: the role of non-linear dynamic systems. *Person-Centered & Experiential Psychotherapies* 10(3): 198–209.

Sommerbeck L (2012) Being non-directive in directive settings. *Person-Centered & Experiential Psychotherapies* 11(3): 173–90.

Speierer G (1990) Towards a specific illness concept of client-centered therapy. In: G Lietaer, J Rombauts, R van Balen (eds) *Client-centered and Experiential Psychotherapy in the Nineties.* Leuven: Leuven University Press.

Swildens, H (2004) Self-pathology and postmodern humanity: challenges for person-centered psychotherapy. *Person-Centered & Experiential Psychotherapies* 3: 4–18.

Szasz T (1961) *The Myth of Mental Illness.* New York: Harper.

Szasz T (1987) *Insanity: The idea and its consequences.* New York: Wiley.

Tudor K (ed) (2008) *Brief Person-Centred Therapies.* London: Sage Publications.

Wyatt G (2001) The multifaceted nature of congruence within the therapeutic relationship. In: G Wyatt (ed) *Rogers' Therapeutic Conditions: Evolution, theory and practice. Vol 1: Congruence.* Ross-on-Wye: PCCS Books.

Zimbardo P (2008) *The Lucifer Effect: Understanding how good people turn evil.* New York: Random House.

Index

9/11 attacks 17

A

acceptance 2, 6, 15–22, 26, 33, 37, 69, 72, 79, 85, 90, 101 (see also 'unconditional positive regard')
accreditation 50
Adams, C 45, 105
assessment
    clinical 61–5, 94
    risk 50, 62–4
auditing 50

B

Baldwin, M 4, 105
Barrett-Lennard, GT 1, 20, 105
benchmarking 50
Bohart , A 83, 84, 105
boundaries 1, 37, 60, 62, 88
Bower, D 22, 77, 83, 105
Bozarth, J 22, 52, 62, 93, 105
brief therapy 69–70
Brodley, BT 1, 15, 73, 74, 75, 80, 82, 88, 89, 90, 95, 105, 106

C

Chicago Counseling Center 8
conditional regard 19, 78, 80, 82–3, 85, 86
confidentiality 37, 53, 54, 68
congruence 3–7, 18, 21, 34, 72, 83, 85–6

contact 4, 6–9, 14–16, 21, 23, 27, 28, 34, 68, 86, 91, 92
    -impaired 9, 21, 92, 107
    work 92
contextual
    limits 49–70
    rules 66
contractual limits 21–3, 40–1, 51, 53, 64
Cooper, M 4, 86, 106, 107
Cooper, D 49, 105
Coulson, Bill 12
Counselling for Depression (CfD) 61, 65, 107
crime 16

D

dependency 33, 35
    counter- 35

devaluation–idealisation dimension 9
diagnosis 61, 64, 65
difficult edge 7, 35
disclosure
    reciprocal 37
    therapist self- 2, 4, 18–19, 54, 80, 85
discrimination 97, 99
Dominic (case study), 4
Dorfman, E 1, 105

E

emotional overwhelm 7, 9

empathic
> mutuality 8
>
> understanding 2, 3, 7–16, 17–19, 32, 33, 37, 43, 45, 69, 71–5, 77, 80–3
>
> responses (EURs) 8, 15, 17, 74, 80

employee assistance programmes 91

Ett, Mrs (Rogers' case) 74, 75

evidence-based practice 50, 65

expert 29, 36, 40, 42, 49, 51, 53, 60, 65, 66, 72, 75, 86–8, 94
> client as 58
>
> -directed psychotherapeutic approaches 51
>
> non- 29, 49–51
>
> -on-the-client 36, 51, 53, 55, 61, 64, 65–6, 69, 72, 76, 99
>
> Rogers as an 75

extra-therapeutic
> competence 97
>
> relationships 1, 2, 21, 59, 88–95

extreme affects 9–14

extreme emotions 9, 10 (see also 'emotional overwhelm')

F

FIN, Mrs (Rogers' case) 27

Frankel, M 3, 6, 7, 71, 72, 80, 83, 84, 105, 106

Frankland, A 2, 107

freedom/determinism 29

friendship relationship 37

G

Gaza 17

Gendlin, E 1, 5, 27, 28, 106, 107

genuineness 29, 45 (see also 'congruence')

Gloria (client) 4, 84

good practice 43
> therapist's judgment of 43

General Practitioner (GP) 53, 54, 58

H

Harrison, M 2, 28, 29, 31, 106

Hart, J 27

holding and letting go 14

homelessness 97

I

idealising clients 10

idiosyncratic limits 2, 45–7, 76

Improving Access to Psychological Treatment (IAPT) 61

incongruence 34, 72, 84, 86
> (see also 'congruence')

internal frame of reference 7, 8

J

Jin Wu 29, 45

K

Kemps, C 73

L

Lietaer, G 1, 5, 28, 74, 105, 106, 108

limit setting 2, 20, 25–47, 49

M

Marion (case study) 55–60, 78, 82

Mearns, D 4, 60, 69, 85, 86, 106

medical model 49–55, 58–61, 65

medication 32, 36, 53, 55, 58, 94, 97

Mendota State Hospital 27

miracle moment 89, 90

moments of movement 69

monologue, client's fast-streaming 15
Moon, K 1, 30, 80, 105, 106
Moorman, J 30
Morgan, D 29, 45

N

Natiello, P 82, 106
necessary and sufficient conditions 83
negative regard 16, 44, 77, 92, 93
non-expert (see 'expert, non')
normalcy 32
number of sessions 68

O

O'Hara, M 69

P

paedophiles/paedophilia 16
PCINTL e-mail network 22, 29, 73
Pearce, P 2, 7, 106
physical illness 97
political factors 92
Pörtner, M 8, 107
poverty 92, 94, 97, 100
pre-therapy 8, 9, 92
prizing the client 20
Proctor, G 92, 93
Prouty, G 8, 107
psychiatrists 54
psychiatry 8, 43, 49–50, 86, 89, 90
    anti- 49
psychosis 7, 10, 32, 64
psychotic 32, 34, 40, 41
psychotic
    episode/experiences 32, 34, 40, 55
    ideation 32, 41

Q

questions
    answering client, 2, 12, 72–84, 92
    inviting 43

R

Rachlin, H 72, 106
red thread 14
referral 2, 69, 91, 93, 97–101
risk assessment (see 'assessment')
Roc, Mrs (Rogers' case) 75
Rogers, CR 1, 3, 4, 5, 6, 7, 8, 10, 11, 12, 13, 14, 15, 16, 17, 19, 20, 21, 25, 26, 27, 28, 29, 31, 37, 39, 43, 44, 47, 49, 61, 72, 73, 74, 75, 76, 80, 82, 83, 84, 85, 86, 87, 88, 93, 103, 105, 106, 107, 108
Rogers-1 3, 106
Rogers-2 3, 106

S

Sachse, R 61
Sanders, P 2, 8, 61, 65, 92, 97, 99, 103, 107
saviour/persecutor/victim triangle 25, 30, 31, 37, 79
schizophrenia 8, 10, 26
self
    -defence 45
    -disclosure, therapist (see 'disclosure')
    -expression 85, 86, 87
sex 26, 28, 37, 46, 74, 82, 90
Shlien, J 2, 22, 69, 107
Shostrom, E 84, 85
Sommerbeck, L 1, 2, 3, 6, 7, 31, 38, 49, 66, 71, 76, 77, 80, 83, 84, 92, 93, 105, 106, 107, 108
Speierer, G 61, 108

Stanford prison experiment 66

suicidal

    ideation 43

    behaviour 38–44, 45, 49

    impulses 32–4, 38, 45, 46, 53, 54, 64

    risk 44, 54, 64

suicide 33, 39, 40, 41, 43

supervision 1, 6, 16, 19, 35, 36, 37, 71, 98

Swildens, H 61

symbolisation 6, 19

symbolised experiences 6, 19

    accurate 6, 19

    innacurate 6, 19

Szasz, T 49

T

Taylor & Francis 49

therapeutic competence, limits of 3–23

therapist

    self-disclosure (see 'disclosure')

    frame of reference 5, 15, 36, 58, 75, 80, 83, 87–8

    transparency (see 'transparency')

Three Approaches to Psychotherapy (film) 4, 106

time-limited therapy 2, 69–70

time out 22, 71–95

Tomlinson, TM 27

transparency 5, 18–19

    therapist 18

Tudor, K 2, 69, 106, 108

U

unconditional

    acceptance 2, 16, 18, 20, 21, 33, 90

    positive regard 3, 14, 16, 17, 19, 20, 22, 30, 31, 43, 45, 82, 83, 106 (see also 'conditional regard')

unemployment 92, 97, 99, 100

V

Van Werde, D 8, 107

violence 49, 90, 97

violent behaviour 36, 44–5, 46

W

WAPCEPC conference 80

Whitaker, C 86

Wilkins, P 2, 107

Wisconsin Project 8, 10, 14, 27, 86–7

Wyatt, G 85, 86, 87, 88, 108

Z

Zimbardo, P 66, 108

Person-Centred Practice at the Difficult Edge

Edited by Peter Pearce and Lisbeth Sommerbeck
2014   ISBN 978 1 906254 69 8

This book presents accounts of the practice of the person-centred approach with difficult client groups such as troubled adolescents, and people suffering from a range of severe and/or enduring conditions. *Person-Centred Practice at the Difficult Edge* comprehensively refutes the notion that person-centred therapy is suitable only for the 'worried well', and backs up contemporary practice with appropriate theory and evidence throughout. Intended for student, academic and professional readerships, it aims to help broaden the range of applications of person-centred practice and encourage interest in working with challenging client groups.

Subject areas include: Autism, adult survivors of childhood sexual abuse, dementia, learning disabilities, palliative care, Pre-Therapy, posttraumatic stress and posttraumatic growth, psychotic process, tenuous contact with adolescents, therapist limits

Contributors: Pamela Bruce-Hay, Mathias Dekeyser, Penny Dodds, Robert Elliott, Jan Hawkins, Stephen Joseph, Danuta Lipinska, David Murphy, Peter Pearce, Hans Peters, Garry Prouty, Anja Rutten, Ros Sewell, Lisbeth Sommerbeck, Sally Stapleton, Wendy Traynor, Dion Van Werde, Margaret Warner

---

The Client-Centred Therapist in Psychiatric Contexts:
A therapists' guide to the psychiatric landscape and its inhabitants
Lisbeth Sommerbeck
2003   ISBN 978 1 898059 55 4

Although client-centred therapy is practised in many medical and psychiatric contexts across Europe, many client-centred therapists are unfamiliar with these settings and client groups. This book is a solid, experience-based attempt to pave the way for mutual respect and greater involvement.

> *It is clearly and beautifully written. Anyone working in a medical or psychiatric context should read this. And anyone working with seriously disturbed clients outside these settings should also read it. To my knowledge, there is no other book like it.*

C.H. 'Pat' Patterson, Professor Emeritus, University of Illinois